NEW 1969 EDITION:

happiness
is a stock that
doubles
in a year

happiness is a stock that doubles in a year

BY IRA U. COBLEIGH

published by

BERNARD GEIS ASSOCIATES

distributed by

GROVE PRESS, INC.

author's note

There are dozens of stocks mentioned, referred to, or briefly described in this book. Information respecting them was taken from sources considered reliable but in no way guaranteed. Moreover, the data concerning any individual issue was necessarily prepared some months ago. Accordingly, if the reader is interested in any of the stocks mentioned for possible purchase, sale, or retention, it is essential that he acquire the latest and most authoritative information about it before making any investment decision. This information should be secured from a responsible broker, dealer, investment adviser, financial publication, or service. In no event is any recommendation or endorsement made of any stock; and nothing herein is to be considered under any circumstance as an offer or inducement to buy, sell, or hold any security at any time.

IRA U. COBLEIGH

contents

NEW 1969 EDITION:

happiness
is a stock that
doubles
in a year

the advantages
and pleasures
of stock speculation

The first edition of *Happiness Is a Stock that Doubles in a Year* was published on July 31, 1967, and became an immediate best seller. It introduced for the first time the theory that stocks that perform spectacularly well, in any year, have certain unique qualities in common. The book went on to isolate and to tabulate those distinguishing features, and reached the logical conclusion that, in any bull-market year, stocks possessing most of these characteristics were far more likely to double than the general run of common stocks.

Finally, to document the validity of this theory, forty-five different issues were screened and listed, with prices as of January 11, 1967, the day after the President delivered his State of the Union address. These forty-five issues had, it was believed, the qualifications for above-average performance, and might even double in 1967. The track record of these selections is set forth in Chapter 1 of this book. Actually, as you will see, fourteen of the issues did double (or better); several came close, and one stock gained 262 points!

This totally new 1969 edition picks up where the other left off. It presents the truly remarkable list of stock issues that doubled on the New York Stock Exchange and the American Stock Exchange during 1967; and offers a more penetrating and sophisticated analysis of the unique qualities possessed by stocks that double. There are many entirely new and highly informative chapters — one on the zooming computer industry and others on conglomerates, leveraged funds, packaged programs, and even a chapter on the fascinating "Hemline Index of Stock Prices," which establishes the novel theory that skirts and stocks go up and down together. This is perhaps the first statistical linking of sex and the stock market! There is a revised chapter on fundamental and technical methods of stock evaluation, plus the Dow Theory; with illustrative bar charts and point and figure charts on two of the most active New York Stock Exchange issues. The chapter on growth stocks has been expanded, and now provides superior criteria for determining whether a given issue is, or is not, a growth stock. Convertible bonds and preferred stocks, discussed in the 1967 edition, are now given full chapter treatment; also warrants, previously included under leverage, are given more intensive coverage in a special new chapter, along with puts and calls.

FOR SPECULATORS ONLY

Again, it should be emphasized that this edition, like its predecessor, is for speculators only! There are in America today about 6.5 million individuals who are avid stock speculators. They take only casual interest in dividends and couldn't care less about bonds (unless they're convertible). But let the conversation drift to Polaroid, Solitron, Data Processing, Wang Laboratories, University Computing, or Monogram Industries, and their eyes will light up! These are the swinging stocks that speculators like — stocks that can move in a hurry, in volume — and that can double in a year! Avid traders search everywhere to uncover stocks like these. They read the financial pages, subscribe to stock magazines and investment services, and swarm into board rooms at lunchtime to watch the numbers click. And they ponder there over speculative commitments they're planning and exult over the swift market-generated gains in their net worth. Stocks well bought and shrewdly traded can not only lead to Rolls-Royces and rubies, but add zest to daily living and forever insulate one from boredom.

This book provides extensive coverage, in the earlier chapters, of the tools to work with: warrants, conglomerates, convertibles, special situations, mergers, take-overs, growth stocks, sleepers, turnaround situations, and market analysis. But most readers will turn rather swiftly — against our advice; we urge you to read these chapters in sequence — to Chapter 18, wherein are boldly set down and discussed forty-five individual stocks believed to offer unusual market potentials for gain — stocks that may even double. No other book on the market is so daring as to even attempt such a list. We had such success, however, with our 1967 selections that we are even more confident about this new list.

This edition of "*Happiness,*" the careful reader will note, places less stress on turnaround industries. Life-insurance and savings-and-loan stocks selected a year ago in that category simply did not live up to their billings and just "sat there" for months on end like tired crows.

We have learned, watching the progress of 'our' 1967 choices, that dynamic stocks in rapidly growing industries go up in general faster and with greater assurance than do stocks of tired companies emerging into strong uptrends in net earnings.

NATURAL RESOURCES

Far more stress has been placed in this edition on natural-resource stocks — issues that represent wealth in the form of minerals, metals, timber and land spreads, and modern buildings, an especially desirable factor in the inflationary period ahead. Sheraton, City Investing, Occidental Petroleum, and Texas Gulf Sulphur were good "resource" examples in the past. There will be others in the future — like Charter Consolidated.

We must caution you that there is no assurance whatever that any stock alluded to may go up. Speculation is still far more of an art than a science, and our crystal ball may cloud up badly at times. To be a helpful guide to speculators, these forecasts will need (1) a bull market of considerable vigor, (2) earnings growth in the industries and issues cited, (3) millions of avid speculators pouring their money into the market, and (4) a lot of luck. This book is a road map, not an insurance policy. You must buy your own gas and do your own driving.

Finally, we would conclude that to speculate rewardingly, you must accent market fashion more than fundamentals, and you must be an informed speculator. Always know something about the stocks you buy and have a good reason for every purchase or sale decision you reach. We have given you documentation, as far as space permits, on every stock we have selected. Furthermore, each issue chosen is backed up by reams of additional research the author has done but just couldn't crowd into these pages. If you've been stupid enough to buy on tips in the past and go on doing it in the future, you were a superdope to pay $6.95 for this book!

Good luck, and may you find that *happiness is a stock that doubles in a year* — especially when you get one that "cooks" like Kentucky Fried Chicken!

1
the 1967 score card

Because *Happiness Is a Stock that Doubles in a Year* presented a totally new approach to speculation, it is only natural that hundreds of readers have inquired, "How did your idea work out? You listed a lot of stocks that you thought, from your 'bench marks,' might double in 1967. Did any of them double? If so, how many?"

Well, as the campaigning senator put it so well, "My friend, I'm glad you asked!"

The 1967 edition did in fact list forty-five stocks selected on the basis that some, at least, might double during the year. The starting point chosen was January 11, the day after President Johnson's State of the Union address. This speech, with a request for a meager 6 percent tax increase, seemed to set the stage for a favorable speculative climate for 1967, and encouraged us to believe that a great many stocks would double — at least! "Well," as the late Governor Al Smith of New York used to say, "let's have a look at the record." Of the forty-five selected for hopeful gain, ten were selling 100 percent or more above the January 11 price at year end. Here they are:

STOCK	1/11/67	12/29/67
General Development	6 1/4	17 5/8
Automatic Sprinkler	27 1/8	72 3/4
Sheraton	10 1/2	29 1/2
Canadian Homestead Oil	2 1/4	4 9/16
Kentucky Fried Chicken	30 1/2	136 1/2
Recognition Equipment	64	169
University Computing	28	290
Univis	20	49 1/2
Data Processing Financial & General	26 1/2	129 1/4
Scurry Rainbow Oil	19 3/4	48 1/2

In addition, the following stocks had more than doubled sometime during the year, although they had slipped off, below the 100 percent gain level, at year end:

STOCK	1/11/67	12/29/67	HIGHEST PRICE IN 1967
Bohack	14 3/4	24	38
Central-Del Rio Oils	13 1/4	22 1/4	26
Cubic	12 3/4	24 1/4	28 1/4
McLean Industries	17	29 3/4	35 1/4

The following issues, while not doubling, displayed their intentions by gaining 50 percent or more:

STOCK	1/11/67	12/29/67
Iowa Beef Packers	34 1/4	53 1/4
Watsco	5 3/4	9
Kaiser Industries	11 3/4	19 1/8
Santa Fe Drilling	29 1/8	44
Alleghany Warrants	6 1/2	10 1/8
Arvida	6	9 3/8
Greatamerica	15 1/4	22 7/8

In summary, fourteen of the forty-five issues mentioned had doubled within the year; and of these, two had gained fourfold and another sevenfold! Seven other issues were selling at least 50 percent higher at year end, and all but seven were selling above their January 11, 1967, prices.

Level investment of an equal number of dollars in each of the forty-five issues would have produced an aggregate gain of 62 percent for the year. This compares with a 15.2 percent rise in 1967 of the Dow-Jones Industrial Average! *Happiness is a stock that doubles in a year* — but a gain of "only" 62 percent would hardly be considered cause for grief.

WHAT ABOUT 1969?

The year 1968 began in a bearish trend and gave indication of postponing any great buoyancy until the closing months. Suddenly, in April, President Johnson announced that he would not run again and asked for preliminary peace talks, and Hanoi sent their diplomats to the negotiating table in Paris. Rumors of peace swarmed all over the market, and by April 15, the Dow-Jones had risen above the 908 high of January 8. All this in the face of gloomy business statistics and an impending steel strike.

Depressed market conditions (prevailing January through March) provided excellent opportunity for bargain-hunting and awaiting the descent of desirable stocks to more attractive price levels. This screening, done with the distinguishing characteristics of stocks that have doubled in the past well in mind, proved worthwhile. Many shares remained low. Marginal gold mines — ones that couldn't earn a profit at $35 an ounce but could prosper if gold reached $70 — were still begging for buyers. You need not stay away from the market when there's a lull in enthusiasm. Bull stocks in bear markets can often be found. Such market climate insists that you stress fundamental values and that you avoid the higher-multiple glamour issues, generally more vulnerable in market downspins. It should be remembered that even in the dull market of early 1968, several gold stocks doubled (Western Deep Levels, Stilfontein, Dome). Possibilities exist in scientific issues, patent-oriented companies, merger baits, and newer industries — oceanography, convalescent homes, lasers. Oil companies that hit new fields can counter a downturn any time.

As you move forward in this 1969 edition, you will find a number of exciting new features:

1. Tabulation of the stocks that doubled in 1967 — hundreds of them!

2. A more complete outline of the historic qualities, or common characteristics, of stocks with potentials of swift advance in any year.

3. A challenging new chapter on speculation in stocks that you don't even own, with a minimum capital outlay: in warrants, puts, and calls.

4. A highly topical chapter on the advantages and pit-

falls of speculating in conglomerates, the glamorous multi-industry companies that have entranced and enriched nimble speculators.

5. A financial first on how to pick stocks in companies that may be "taken over" — "The Corporate Hunter and his Quarry."

6. A potentially rewarding road map to the possibilities in "hot" new issues, and how to subscribe to them — early!

7. Finally, there appears a list of dynamic stocks winnowed from hundreds of others, selected because they appear to have those special qualities making them far more likely to double in 1968-69 than the stocks picked at random for speculative gain.

We ought to say, in this chapter, a few words about the stocks that didn't "make it" last year. The savings-and-loan stocks we recommended — Great Western, Financial Federation, and First Charter — didn't do a thing in 1967, although in the spring they had seemed certain to advance. They waited perversely and by April 8, 1968, had scored gains of 50 to 70 percent over 1967 year-end closings. We were apparently on the right track but 1967 just wasn't a long enough year.

Life-insurance shares, though they continued to increase their earnings by 7 percent or more annually, simply didn't attract a following, and they wound up the year at about the same prices they started, or lower. We're convinced that they'll live up to their billing in 1968-69, and you'll see in Chapter 18 five life stocks that we consider well worth singling out.

2

the rules of the game and fundamentals of stock selection

Our object in this book is to seek out undervalued stocks and to so time their purchase as to realize capital gains on them of 100 percent or more within the ensuing twelve months. Vital to success in such a program are techniques of valuation or appraisal that can indicate, with some accuracy, when a stock is underpriced and at what level it offers promise of a significant gain in price. The oldest and most respected technique for analysis of stock values is the fundamental method.

THE BASIC INGREDIENTS

The fundamental approach centers around the axiom "Stock prices are the slaves of earning power." Over a period of time, stocks tend (1) to rise quite faithfully in response to increases in earnings (and to decline when earnings slip) and (2) to increase in their price/earnings multiples while earnings gain.

Look at the recent earnings' growth of such leaders as IBM, McGraw-Hill, Texas Instruments, Occidental Petroleum, Polaroid, and Kentucky Fried Chicken and you will find, in every instance, a rate of growth in net earnings far above that of the average corporation; and you will find that this rate of growth was translated into dramatic gains in the prices of the stocks.

The rise in stock prices in response to a favorable profit trend is seldom precisely parallel to it. Share prices in issues that have attracted an enthusiastic market following have in fact often risen at far steeper rates than the related earnings, on occasion reaching quite dazzling price/earnings multiples of 60 or more.

EARNINGS AS PROPELLANTS

A study of earning power is the backbone of the fundamental method of security appraisal. A rising long-term trend in earnings is an almost certain clue to a stock that will advance in the market. However, in some industries (cyclical ones, such as building materials, copper, machine tools), earnings may rise rapidly for a time, only to fall off sharply, and it is vital to note when these changes in direction take place. Some companies will show reduced earnings in a year, due perhaps to large outlays for plant expansion or research of a new product. This also must be taken into account, because in the following year these capital investments may result in net earnings at an all-time high.

For example, some excellent electric-utility stocks and life-insurance-company shares recorded no significant price gains (and some actual declines) between

1964 and the spring of 1968, yet during this period their earnings and dividends advanced without a pause to new highs. These conservative or defensive-type investments simply failed, during the time span in question, to attract enthusiastic buying, not because their statistics were unfavorable — quite the contrary — but because the issues generated no market "oomph," and gain-minded traders preferred to purchase stocks that were (1) more active on the tape, (2) more glamorous (and speculative) in nature, and (3) in shorter supply. We conclude, therefore, that when rising earnings were insufficient market propellants, the issues were either (1) too high-priced earlier and stabilized at lower levels, (2) not sufficiently glamorous to attract a following of "swinging" speculators, or (3) awaiting a time when sound dividend-paying stocks again became fashionable among market operators.

Earnings are, moreover, a two-way street, and if stocks go up when earnings rise, they also go down when earnings fall. (Examples: American Motors in 1966, the savings-and-loan and cement stocks in 1965-66, Litton and Automatic Sprinkler in 1967-68.)

GROWTH FACTORS

Not only rising earnings but general growth in sales and assets as well are important fundamental factors influencing stock prices. Rates of growth are especially important. A company doubling its sales in five years, with a corresponding increase in net, will surely have a stock with a rising market trend. Companies whose sales and earnings have grown at the rate mentioned, or even a better rate, have indeed attracted strong market followings. Examples of companies growing in this manner would include Data Processing Financial and General, Litton, American Hospital Supply, Gulf & Western Industries, Occidental Petroleum, Belco Petroleum, Lum's, University Computing, and Sterling Electronics.

THE MANAGEMENT FACTOR

We would not be covering fundamental methods of analysis at all well if we didn't say something about management. How many great companies do we know that are the lengthened shadows of enormously gifted and energized individuals? Can you imagine the Ford Motor Company without the pioneer genius of Henry Ford; Helena Rubenstein without the amazing skills of its founder; Litton Industries if "Tex" Thornton hadn't come along; IBM with the Watsons absent; Republic National Life without Theodore Beasley; Combined Insurance without Clement Stone; Occidental Petroleum without Armand Hammer; Perkin-Elmer minus Richard Perkin? Of course, a big corporation today is not a one-man band, but it is important to note how many great companies have become industrial titans because of their leadership by individuals endowed with remarkable amounts of initiative, imagination, drive, and guts. Outstandingly competent business virtuosi are not always recognized in early corporate phases; and the big trend today is to run the show by management teams, with each member having considerable autonomy in his own department or division. Alfred Sloan's excellent book, *My Years with General Motors*, outlines splendidly the development of corporate efficiency under a team of division managers, with considerable interdivision competition.

Admittedly the qualities of good management are hard to define; but they are fairly easy to document. In general, quality management is evidenced by rising sales, the introduction and marketing of new products or services, improving profit margins, and especially the increase of profits at a faster rate than sales. The ultimate test of management is the conversion of sales into net profits. Thus, in any given industry, look for the company with the best growth rate in gross income, the highest ratio of net profits to sales volume, and the highest returns on invested capital. These relationships will vary, of course, from industry to industry and company to company; and you can't compare statistical ratios between a railroad and a department store, or an electronics and an insurance company. But within any industry you can compare results, year by year, broken down by quarters, and the best results at the cash register are almost invariably reported by the best-managed companies.

OTHER FUNDAMENTAL FACTORS

Other fundamental factors have an important bearing on the thrust and direction of stock prices. These include such items as balance-sheet positions (current position and debt structure); a calculation and comparison of profit margins; percentages earned on invested capital and on net worth (stockholders' equity); cash flow; and dividend payments. Further, a review of current and past annual reports may prove revealing. Observation of changes in sales, expenditures for research, development of new products or services, acquisition programs, and changes in dividend payments will round out the valuation procedure.

Price/earnings multiples are usually significant, and comparisons of these ratios with those of other companies in the same industry are often useful.

The most successful companies will display two important earnings characteristics: (1) their net earnings will increase year by year (the rapidly growing ones may increase their net profits 15 percent or more annually), and (2) their earnings will grow at a faster rate than their sales. Seek out companies with these characteristics and you're quite likely to find shares with potentials for unusual market gain.

A high price/earnings multiple is often an index of

outstanding quality or unusual growth potential or both
(IBM, Xerox, and Polaroid all sell consistently at multiples of 40 or higher). These ratios are, however, somewhat confusing because they're constantly changing.
Generally, P/E ratios rise during bull markets and fall
in bear ones; but if a company's earnings dive in a given
year, the subject stock may actually sell at a substantially
higher than normal multiple of (lower) per share earnings.

FUNDAMENTALS IN GENERAL

The fundamental approach to security values includes
not only the analysis of industrial and corporate statistics
outlined here but a consideration of prevailing political
and economic conditions as well. Credit conditions and
the supply and price (interest rate) of money are vital
factors. In the early stages of bull markets, money is usually both plentiful and cheap. Companies borrow for
corporate expansion, and individuals borrow increasingly
to buy securities. New plant additions and expansions
tend to increase corporate earnings, and stocks respond
to the higher earning power by going up. It is in this early
phase of a bull market, of course, that the most attractive
purchasing opportunities in common stocks appear. However, in this stage (which often follows a period of recession), many investors either are timid because they are
mindful of fairly recent market losses, or lack available
funds for aggressive speculation. This tentative attitude
toward the market fades as stocks advance, and as the
incomes of individuals and corporations advance. The
years 1960-66 powerfully illustrate the economic upsurge
we have just described, which led to the next market
stage, wherein money supply and credit availability
played key roles. In March, 1968, the Federal Reserve
rediscount rate was advanced from 4.5 to 5 percent, and
at the same time general interest rates were around the

highest levels in forty years. Blue-chip stocks yielded only 50 percent of the income yields of high-grade corporate bonds; banks throughout the land were charging 6 percent and more on individual loans, and credit became progressively restrictive. This monetary situation had the predictable effect of slowing down stock buying, and the market sold off over 15 percent on the Dow-Jones Industrial Average (DJIA) in the first quarter of 1968.

The stiffening of credit availability and rates (often accompanied by increased margin requirements) has historically tended to put a brake on market enthusiasm, and both credit and margins are basic elements in the fundamental analysis of securities.

FUNDAMENTAL VALIDITY

Most sophisticated investors, individual and institutional, agree that knowledge and appraisal of the fundamental factors we cited provide vital guidelines to the selection of dynamic stocks. These are the logical factors bearing upon the evaluation of stocks, and are the basic tools of those who invest for sustained income and long-term growth. But changing psychology often has a greater bearing on the current stock quotations than statistical changes with a company or industry. In fact, many experts believe that market action is 40 percent logical and 60 percent psychological.

As long as America is a land of free enterprise, our stock market will continue to be a huge, animate auction center, where buyers and sellers of securities meet and exchange views on values. While the rise and fall of prices will always be related to corporate earnings and dividends, it will also be influenced by the ever shifting attitudes, psychological whims, and caprices of the public.

Therefore, in our endeavor to winnow winners from some 34,000 different stock issues traded with some frequency in the listed and over-the-counter markets, we must take into proper consideration both the impact of human emotions and corporate arithmetic in projecting the prices of shares. Stock prices can sometimes be slaves as much to emotions as to earning power.

USES OF TECHNICAL ANALYSIS

The fundamental approach is not satisfactory to the "quick buck" boys; the guidance given, and the possible clues to action stocks supplied by these fundamentals are too languid and too inert. True, a given stock with a strong uptrend in net earnings will probably advance over time; but it may take a year or two before the public is sufficiently aware of this upthrust in earnings to move the stock significantly. Moreover, in a market sell-off, such as occurred in the spring of 1968, fundamentally strong stocks with dynamic earnings went down with the rest. Anyway, two years is too long a wait for an impetuous speculator. So the quick-profit trader seeks methods of winnowing out stocks that may shortly advance, for reasons not found in their earnings reports or dividend declarations. Many stocks go up just because they have attracted a following and become fashionable.

One of the popular methods for perceiving in advance the possible direction of stock prices is called technical analysis. This attempts to study the day-by-day performance of individual stocks, and of the market as a whole, by careful analysis of daily volumes of trading and price movements. Technical analysis endeavors to discern, from past performance of active stocks, or from market averages such as the Dow-Jones Industrial Average, the indicated future trends. It is based on the aforementioned theory that market movements are more psychological than logical phenomena. Often a stock

will go up without any significant change in its fundamental values, simply because a heavier flow of the
public's money enters the issue. This condition is evident when (1) the daily trading volume in the stock increases noticeably above average volume for the preceding thirty days, and (2) when this increase in volume
is accompanied by higher price quotations and, especially,
new "highs." Conversely, when volume increases above
recent daily averages, with a *downtrend* in price, the
message is that the public is moving out of that issue;
that its sale is indicated; and that a further price decline
may be expected.

NEED FOR CHARTS

To record and analyze this price-and-volume data,
charts are essential. There are two principal kinds —
bar charts and point-and-figure charts.

Bar Charts. The most popular is called a bar chart. It
may cover transactions for a day, a week, a month, or a
year. Customarily, the horizontal scale, running from left
to right, will be the time scale covering the period included; while the vertical scale will represent the price
changes. If the chart is of ordinary squares, or cross-
section paper, both the horizontal (time) scale and the
vertical (price) scale will be uniform. The distance on the
chart will be the same between a price of 10 and 20 as
between 90 and 100.

Most market "pros," however, prefer a logarithmic or
scale chart. This has a larger space or distance between
prices at lower levels than at higher ones. The reason for
using a scale that shrinks as prices rise is to bring price
changes into perspective and to facilitate percentage comparisons. For example, if a stock moves from 10 to 20, it
has gained 100 percent; but if it moves from 50 to 60 (also
10 points), it has gained but 20 percent. Since it's the

percentage gain that is important, the "log" chart is superior, since each advance of, say, 10 percent will represent the same vertical distance on the chart whether the actual price movement is from 10 to 11 or from 100 to 110.

Plotting the chart is pretty well standardized. You connect the day's high and the day's low by a vertical line, and the closing price is shown by a very short horizontal line crossing the vertical one. You plot in the same data each succeeding day, and shortly you will have a chart that shows a trend—which is what we're really looking for.

About volume: that is usually shown on a special scale running along the bottom of the page; and many precise individuals also make notes at the bottom indicating when stocks sell ex dividend, ex rights, pay extra dividends, stock dividends, and so on. There is no sense, however, in keeping charts unless they're up to date. If you're going to plot the charts yourself, you should be a neat, patient, and mathematically-minded individual. Otherwise, you should probably get the charts you want, on the issues that interest you, from Dines, Trendline, Mansfield, M. C. Horsey, or one of the other services. Many investment services and market letters of leading stock-exchange firms illustrate by bar charts market action in individual stocks and in the whole market.

If you prefer doing the charts yourself, get the proper equipment: the right pen or pencil, a triangle, a ruler, folders for the charts; and have a well-lighted table or desk at which to work. Keep everybody (particularly children) away from your desk so that your charts won't get messed up. Don't try to chart twenty stocks a day. If you get behind, you'll never catch up. Try no more than four or five for openers. You have a choice of time periods. A weekly or a monthly chart is best for most speculators looking for short- or intermediate-term trends.

These charts provide valuable information. First, they reveal what people were actually willing to pay or take for a given stock on given days. This is the real value of any stock — what it will fetch on the market. Emotion or mass psychology, rather than reason, may have dictated the prices recorded, but the prices do not lie. Your chart reveals what has been called "the bloodless verdict of the marketplace."

A collection of these weekly or monthly charts strung together may reveal a strong directional trend. In the cases of companies whose earnings are rising steadily in each succeeding quarter, you may observe a steady upward slope on the chart. It need not be an uptrend in earnings that provides the propulsion. The same upslant might result if the stock were steadily under accumulation for any cause.

To illustrate the graphic account of market changes revealed by bar charts, we have shown the charts of Occidental Petroleum and Control Data in 1967, as well as a chart of the DJIA.

BAR CHART — DJ INDUSTRIAL AVERAGE — 1967

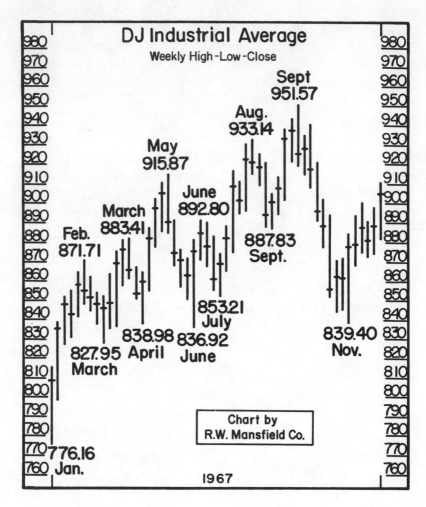

BAR CHART — OCCIDENTAL PETROLEUM — 1967

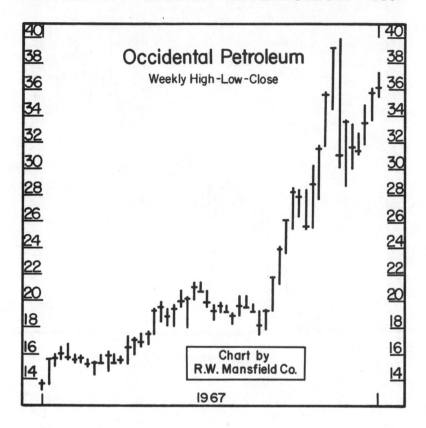

Occidental Petroleum
Weekly High-Low-Close

Chart by
R.W. Mansfield Co.

1967

BAR CHART — CONTROL DATA — 1967

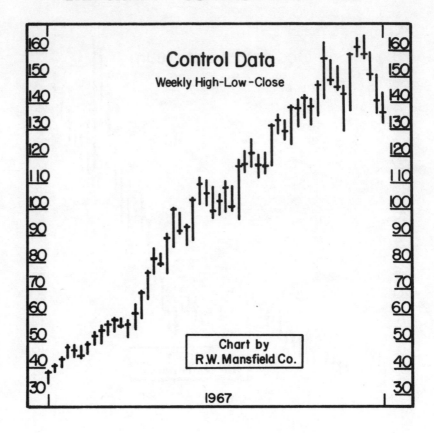

We can't begin to cover here all the things you should notice in chart analysis: reversals, breakouts, boxes, rectangles, "head and shoulder" formations, consolidations, etc. Your real goal is to define and discern a trend. It is defined by a line connecting the bottoms of at least two (and preferably more) reactions in a stock that has been advancing. In such a case, this line (called a trendline) should slant upward. Connecting the "tops" of two or more rallies when a stock is declining may define a trendline on the down side. This all sounds a bit complicated — and it is. If you really want to place reliance on charts to guide your buying and selling, you'd better get a professional book or two on the subject — possibly the one on *Technical Analysis* by Edwards and Magee. But from what we've given here, you should be able to look at a representative bar chart and derive some sort of message from it. The more you learn about charts, the more revealing will be the message.

Most stocks perform erratically, surging to peaks, dropping back, then surging ahead again, with the pivot zones called support or resistance areas. Many pros are convinced that each stock develops its own unique pattern; and that trends recorded in the past may be expected to recur with considerable fidelity at a later date. From this historical perspective, traders often feel they can estimate with some accuracy how far up or down a stock will go in a given "move."

Point-and-Figure Charts. Another type of chart, used less frequently, is the point-and-figure chart. Here a uniform chart paper is used, with each box or square representing a unit of price. Customarily, each square will represent 1 point in the price of a stock, although in shares selling below 20, each box may represent only ½ point. Price changes, to be recorded on the chart, must cover at least three squares up or down. The letter X is customarily used to denote up moves and 0 down moves.

Trendlines are not drawn until a bullish formation or a bearish formation has appeared. Then the trendline will be constructed quite arbitrarily at an angle of 45 degrees (either up or down). Stocks are thought to be in a buying range when actual sales are above the trendline; and in a selling phase when the trading takes place at prices below the trendline.

Point-and-figure charts do not concern themselves with a time factor. They simply record changes in price, and aim to reveal the supply-and-demand factors affecting a given stock. The theory is that if demand is strong (more powerful than supply), then the stock will continue to go up until supply (selling) is more insistent. Then the stock will decline. Key patterns on point-and-figure charts are triple-top and triple-bottom formations and bullish or bearish triangles.

Point-and-figure savants, after they have arrived at a reasonably well-marked trendline, often use a quite simple formula for "counting" the market to determine the probable immediate or intermediate price objective of a given stock. They count the number of squares (across) used in building the chart pattern, and multiply that by 3 (because it takes a move of at least three squares at a time to define a trend reversal). The product thus reached is, theoretically, the forthcoming nearby or intermediate price objective of the subject stock. This "count" will indicate the probable price the stock you've been watching should reach in a forthcoming rally, but it won't tell you *when* that price will be reached.

For delving into point-and-figure charts, Chartcraft Inc. prepares charts in profusion on individual stocks each week; and it also can supply a booklet or brochure describing major features of P&F analysis.

These charts should be regarded as useful adjuncts and cross checks to price valuations arrived at by other methods.

1967 POINT-AND-FIGURE CHART
Based on daily highs and lows
Occidental Petroleum
(1 x 3 point Reversal Chart)

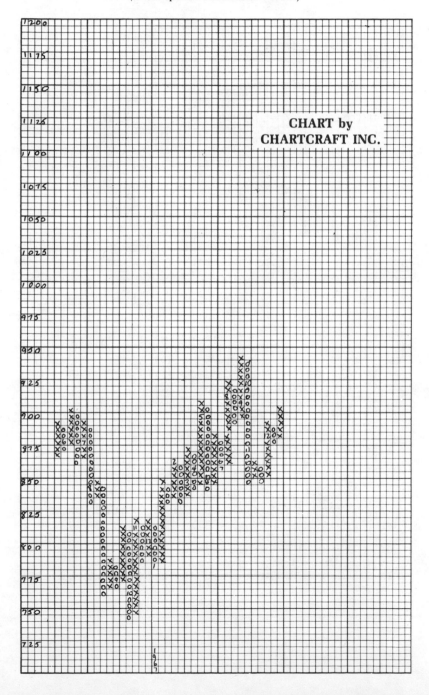

1967 POINT-AND-FIGURE CHART
Based on daily highs and lows
Control Data Corporation
(1 x 3 point Reversal Chart)

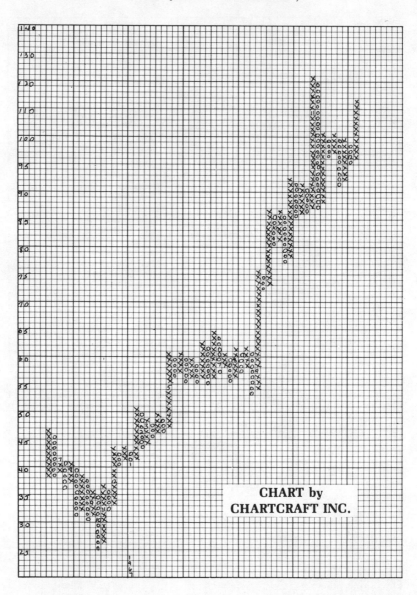

CHART by
CHARTCRAFT INC.

1967 POINT-AND-FIGURE CHART
Based on 11, 12, 1, 2 and closing prices
The Dow-Jones Industrial Average
(A 5 x 15 point Reversal Chart)

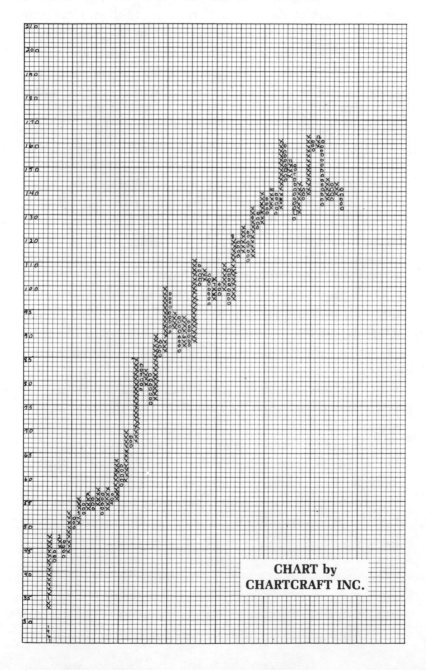

CHART by
CHARTCRAFT INC.

MOVING AVERAGES

Another sophisticated technical procedure is the moving average. This is calculated on bar charts and is obtained by adding together closing prices on a given stock for a number of days (three, five, or ten) and dividing the sum by the number of units traded in the same period. This gives an average price; and if you calculate a new average every three days, and plot these averages on a chart, you get a moving average or trendline. In an active market period, this moving-average method will point to the direction in which stocks are moving, but it is less informative as to when the top or bottom of a swing is at hand, and is inconclusive in horizontal price patterns. Standard use relates moving averages to regular price trends, with both plotted on the same bar chart. Buying or selling signals are given when moving-average lines cross price-pattern lines. All this, however, is rather complicated and of little practical use unless you dote on mathematics and are a chart bug.

All of these technical approaches are designed (1) to define trendlines and (2) to give guidance for proper action by pointing the way to significant trend changes. But these systems, charts, volume studies, moving averages, and the rest depend in great part on the skill, judgment, and experience of the person who interprets the data. The mathematics may be right but the conclusions wrong!

Many active traders who on occasion get stocks that double place great reliance on some form of technical analysis; but unless you are, or become, a gifted and hard-working chartist, you'll probably do just as well if you derive inspiration on market timing from other sources.

THE DOW THEORY

The Dow Theory is based on the premise that rising and falling markets correspond quite faithfully to levels of business activity as revealed in a representative index of industrial production. This Dow hypothesis has fascinated market speculators because (1) stock markets operate in up and down trends which may actually predict and project their directions, often months ahead; and (2) the stock market can act as an advance barometer of general business conditions. In acceptance of this theory, there is wide belief today that a significant decline in the stock market may foretell a decline in business activity, and in profits, a few months or a year later. Equally, strong bull markets moving toward new highs are thought to herald the tidings of good business for many months in the future.

Without attempting to list all the changes in the individual issues comprising these averages over the years, we are setting down below the component issues in the Dow-Jones Industrial Averages (DJIA) and the Dow-Jones Railroad Averages (DJRA) in 1968.

THE 30 DOW-JONES INDUSTRIALS

Allied Chemical	International Nickel
Aluminum Company of America	International Paper
American Can	Johns-Manville
American Telephone & Telegraph	Owens-Illinois
American Tobacco	Procter & Gamble
Anaconda	Sears, Roebuck
Bethlehem Steel	Standard Oil (Calif.)
Chrysler	Standard Oil (N.J.)
Du Pont	Swift
Eastman Kodak	Texaco
General Electric	Union Carbide
General Foods	United Aircraft
Goodyear	U.S. Steel
International Harvester	Westinghouse Electric
	Woolworth

THE 20 DOW-JONES RAILS	
Atchison, Topeka & Santa Fe	Louisville & Nashville
Atlantic Coast Line	New York Central
Canadian Pacific	Norfolk & Western
Chesapeake & Ohio	Pennsylvania
Chicago & North Western	Seaboard Air Line
Delaware & Hudson	St. Louis-San Francisco
Denver & Rio Grande Western	Southern Pacific
Great Northern	Southern Railway
Illinois Central	Union Pacific
Kansas City Southern	Western Pacific

Reduced to its simplest elements, the Dow Theory operates on the principle that the market tells its own story and prophesies its own future. By combining in one place (the stock exchange) the opinions, the estimates, and the judgments of all the people who buy and sell each day, the market is thought, in its own mystical way, to be foretelling the future. The ups and downs in the Dow-Jones averages do far more than indicate or reflect the earning power, dividend payments, and prospects of individual companies. They bear a barometric relationship to things to come. Accordingly, if your goal is to double your money by prudent and timely purchase of the right stocks, some knowledge and application of the Dow Theory may be not only useful but quite possibly rewarding.

HOW IT WORKS

The best practical exposition of this whole subject is Robert Rhea's *The Dow Theory*, written in 1932, and his subsequent book, *Dow Theory Revised*, which amplifies the first book. If you want to become deeply indoctrinated in Dow, then read these works by Rhea.

The market is, like an ocean, always in motion. Movements are, according to the Dow Theory, threefold. There are first the day-to-day price movements, relatively narrow and not particularly revealing so far as any trend is concerned. The second movement is a middle-range one, often lasting for a month or two; and the third may last from three to five or more years — a full-scale bull or bear market, as the case may be. Obviously, the third movement creates the peaks or valleys, with the earlier part of this phase generating the most dramatic price swings.

The most important thing to determine is the primary long-term movement — the full-scale bull or bear market, which historically has ranged from two to six years.

The second element in the Dow Theory is what is called the secondary reaction. No bull market rises without interruption — a plateau or a setback — and no bear market declines without some intermediate rallies. Thus, these secondary reactions are important not only as brakes, or corrections, to major trends, but they are tricky and sometimes seem to indicate that a bull or bear market is at an end when, in truth, it is not. For example, the market break in May-June, 1962, eroded the DJIA by almost 30 percent, and some investors thought that this ended the bull market. Actually, the sell-off from 734.91 (a then all-time high) on December 12, 1961, and 146 in the Railroad average, to May 28 lows of 576.93 and 122.35, respectively, turned out to be merely a very energetic secondary reaction, an interlude in the bull market, which later soared, on February 9, 1966, to 995.15. The thing to note in this example of mid-1962 was the way in which the Rail average "confirmed" the action of the DJIA. Usually this confirming or "me, too" relationship of the Rail average is a somewhat lagging one. Most of the time the DJIA will lead the trendline, while the Rails tag along to confirm, or fail to deny, the correctness and validity of the direction indicated by the senior average.

Secondary reactions require skill for their detection. They generally last for three to four months and, on the average, will retrace about 50 percent of the price changes which have occurred since the end of the preceding secondary reaction. On charts, these reactions represent jagged lines which modify a long-range up- or downtrend.

The daily fluctuations in prices are given little value in the Dow Theory. It's the primary trends and secondary reactions that tell the tale. And Dow attaches great importance to the action of the Industrials and Rails in concert. A primary trend or a secondary reaction in DJIA is not official unless confirmed by the DJRA.

All of these market motions are revealed by charts which you'll find daily in *The Wall Street Journal* and in a number of financial journals and investment-service letters. Many Dow fans like to keep their own charts, but this is not recommended unless you have a lot of time to devote to it, and are mathematically-minded and meticulously accurate.

The most important markers in determining the primary trend are the making of new tops or bottoms in a current cycle. If, for example, the market reaches a new high and in its next decline stops at a point above the low points recorded in an earlier phase, then a bull market is indicated, and the chart may be expected in coming weeks to sawtooth to higher levels. Equally, if a previous low is penetrated, and the ensuing rally stops below the preceding high point, then a bear signal has been clearly given.

When the price movements of both DJIA and DJRA move in parallel and within a narrow price range (not more than 6 percent variation) for ten days or longer, this is called a line and its direction provides another classic Dow guideline. If this line points up, you may assume stocks are being accumulated (bullish). If the line is a downtrend, then you have evidence of distribution (bearish). There are some related theories, too, about volume: when volume dries up on rallies and increases on declines, a bear trend is indicated; and, conversely, when the market is listless on declines but in active volume on upturns, it's bullish. There is also a theory that all bull markets end with a roar—a selling climax with 14 to 20 million shares in daily volume.

The foregoing is obviously only a basic exposition of the Dow Theory. It is designed only as an outline; and if the theory really fascinates you, then read books on the subject, or seek out one of the market services that specialize in Dow technology.

HOW GOOD IS DOW?

There is a steady running argument among speculators about the validity and usefulness of the Dow Theory. On the record, it apparently called the end of the bear market in mid-1932, foretold the end of the bull market in 1937, and blew the big whistle on the market in 1929. The rise in 1961 was outlined by a number of Dow charts. In August, 1962, a very clear call for a bull-market resumption was shown by Dow, and throughout 1964 the Dow signals were all bullish. A number of Dow followers believed that their charts defined the end of the bull market in May, 1966, and the uptrend in the first ten months of 1967.

Many traders have complained that Dow provides its signals too late. By the time the Dow bull or bear signals have been confirmed, they contend, a substantial part of the price swing has already occurred, reducing the profit potentials of commitments then made. Another criticism of Dow is that the Railroad average has lost its historic usefulness as a confirming factor, since transportation is a much broader industry today, embracing private cars, buses, airlines, pipelines, etc. Moreover, railroads are rigidly regulated. Finally, critics say that thirty stocks are too few to represent the action of the whole market; and that certain stocks with notable growth characteristics have quite disregarded the Dow trendline. Different issues in the DJIA would also have changed its course dramatically. If, for example, IBM had been included instead of AT&T, the DJIA today would be several hundred points higher!

Obviously this is no complete critique of the Dow Theory. We would conclude that, as a forecaster, it has served us with considerable accuracy for over three generations; that while not perfect or infallible in appraisal of bull and bear swings over the years, it has been more often right than wrong; and that its major and most powerful signals proved either protective or profitable. In any event, it is helpful to use this system in verifying market trends defined by other techniques. Dow is, at the very least, a distinctly useful tool.

3

recognizing the right time for the right stock

As you will see from the tabulations in later chapters, stocks that have doubled in the past were far more numerous in those years in which the market climate was favorable — when controlling statistical tables of corporate earnings, per capita incomes, new business formations, and the Gross National Product were all in a strong uptrend.

Accordingly, it may be useful to spend a little time on trends, since they exert so important an influence on stock prices. Taking the long view, there are two trends we're pretty certain about. One is the growth trend. We have come to expect in America that every succeeding decade will carry our country to new high levels in agricultural and industrial production, population, corporate earnings and industrial incomes, and revenues from taxes. Therefore, because our entire business, government, agricultural, and service sectors are constantly expanding, we're a confident nation — an eternally bullish nation. In stock speculation, the overwhelming majority opinion, over any period of years, is bullish. We may be bearish for the short term, on account of strikes, a recession, rumors of wars, possible currency devaluation, and the like; but taking the long view, 85 percent of all Americans (and 100 percent of all stockbrokers) expect the market to go up, indefinitely.

Supplementing a built-in growth factor as a market propellant is another of equal long-term validity — inflation. This is a fancy economic word with many definitions, but what we really mean by it is that, year by year, the purchasing power of the dollar is going down. In 1968, it will buy less than half what it would have bought in 1945, at the end of World War II.

This inflationary trend is one we can count on to continue unceasingly, barring a major depression. Why? Because of the inexorable annual increases in: (1) the cost of government; (2) the rise in debt of (a) national, state, and local governments, (b) corporations, and (c) individuals; and (3) the constant annual rise in the price of labor. These three things together assure us that year by year the combined costs will cause rising prices for everything. Rising prices mean that our dollar will continue to buy less. Thus we not only expect the prices of clothing, houses, motorcars, groceries, and medical services to go up, but we expect stock prices to go up as well. They will have to, because corporate earnings and assets are not reported in constant dollars but in ever shrinking ones.

To document the upthrusts created by our steady corporate and governmental growth rates and the steady march of inflation, observe the consistent forward motion in the Dow-Jones Industrial Average to ever higher plateaus:

DATE	DJIA MILESTONE	CLOSING AVERAGE
12/30/49	Crossed 200 for first time since 8/21/46	200.52
3/22/54	Crossed 300	301.60
1/3/55	Topped 400	408.89
3/12/56	Topped 500	500.24
12/18/57	Indonesia nationalized Dutch business and market hit a cyclical low	426.18
1/4/60	Big rebound as steel companies settled 120-day strike	679.06
10/25/60	Cuba confiscated $1.5 billion in American properties	566.05
5/17/61	Dow topped 700	706.52
12/31/61	Historic Dow high	734.91
6/26/62	Four-year low	536.27
11/6/62	Buoyant recrossing of the 600 mark	610.48
2/26/64	$11.5 billion tax reduction	799.38
2/9/66	All-time Dow high	995.15
1/11/67	Day after President's State of Union speech	822.49
1/1/68	January high	908.92
4/15/68	Rebound after three-month dip	910.19

After selling above 900 in early 1968, the market sold off heavily to a March low of 825; but in the first fifteen days of April, it regained all of its lost ground, buoyed by prospects for peace in Vietnam and by the solution (for the time being) of the gold problem. (The largest volume in history, 20,410,000 shares, was recorded on April 10, 1968.)

From this short catalogue of market changes, you can see, beyond question, that the long-term stock price trend is up, with, of course, backing and filling along the way. The market never goes straight up or straight down; it woggles.

In addition to rising corporate earnings and prospects, market uptrends are definitely stimulated by (1) tax reductions, (2) reductions in rediscount rates, (3) reductions in margin requirements, and (4) settlement of major strikes. Conversely, increases in taxes, rediscount rates, and margins, and imminence of major strikes are generally bearish. (On April 20, 1968, when the rediscount rate was increased from 5 to 5½ percent, the DJIA sold off 11.6 points on that day.) These factors are important to consider in making speculative decisions. You can buy the most attractive stock on the Board, but it will have a hard time moving up if the general market is in a visible bearish trend, or depressed by bearish news. The prospect of war is always bearish because it intimates a quite regimented economy with wage and price controls, higher taxes, and excess-profits taxes.

Markets of greater volume and volatility than in the past are also ordained by the facts that about 33 percent of all trading on the New York Stock Exchange is now for the accounts of institutional investors, and many mutual funds turn over one-third of their portfolios each year.

Trends are important not only in the total market but in individual industries as well. Even in the most prosperous times there are leading and laggard industries. Our task, granted a generally encouraging market climate, is (1) to pick the uptrending industries and (2) to acquire the most dynamic issues within them.

History offers little guidance here, and we gain no real benefit from knowing that airlines and televisions were "hot" in 1965; that televisions, oils, computers, and conglomerates were roaring in 1967. What we want to know is what are the dominant trends in industry ahead. If we have peace, then building shares may be market winners: cement, realty, lumber, aluminum, savings-and-loan companies. Issues in this sector might include Kaiser Industries, Ideal Basic, Uris Buildings, General Development, Royal Inns, Georgia-Pacific, Lone Star Cement, Financial Federation, etc.

We must also observe the nationwide clamor for measures to overcome the pollution of our water and air and, as stock traders, we expect to find winning stocks in those categories. We're constantly seeking energy sources; so the oil drillers, nuclear- and thermal-energy companies should be on our list. Also, we face a whole new technology in oceanography. Companies in that field should obviously be considered. Not to get ahead of ourselves, since our specific recommendations are reserved for later, we might mention that in the field of oceanography there is a company that is not particularly well known but is developing broad capabilities: Sterling Electronics. And of course, the most obvious oceangoing stocks at the moment are the offshore oil drillers.

TIMING

So much for trends. Even within them, however, timing is important, so we should say a few things about that. If you've picked an industry and a representative stock in it, you still have to answer the question of when to buy it. Should you buy it immediately or await a more propitious moment? No one really knows the answer to this, but there are some general observations from the past that may help.

First, bad or unpredictable news usually exerts no lasting effect on the market. For example, the market recovered 100 percent of its losses from the following events within a relatively short period:

EVENT	NUMBER OF DAYS TO RECOVERY OF MARKET LEVEL PREVAILING IMMEDIATELY PRIOR TO EVENT
Munich Crisis, 1938	64
Czechoslovakian Crisis, 1939	154
Korean Crisis, 1950	56
President Eisenhower's Illness, 1955	37
Cuban Crisis, 1962	12

In the wake of shocking or disturbing events, the market invariably sells off emotionally; but after evaluation (unless there's a full-scale war), prices will generally snap back within a few weeks. Don't press the panic button.

Politics has little long-run market effect. Who's in the White House or what party is in power is not a factor you can calculate in your timing of security purchases.

There is little statistical evidence that there are any regular or dependable "summer rallies." There is strong evidence, however, that if the stock market rises in January, it will rise for the year. In the past thirty years, a rising January has meant a rising year over 70 percent of the time; and a falling January has meant lower prices for the year on about the same percentage basis.

Year-end (December) rallies seem to occur more than 65 percent of the time but are still not a sure bet. The most valid adage is that the market never discounts the same thing twice.

The foregoing notes about trends and timing may prove valuable to you. Everyone recognizes that correct timing in any endeavor in life is one of the greatest assurances of success. It certainly is in stocks!

4

fortune-building computers

The fastest-growing major industry today is the computer industry, and every long-term investor and gain-seeking speculator should busy himself gathering information about the exciting technological advances and some of the amazing growth companies in this field. One might even call 1967 the year of the computer. Almost every active stock in this market sector at least doubled in 1967, and several issues multiplied investor dollars in an even more dramatic manner. Control Data ranged in 1967 from 33½ to 165⅝; University Computing from 30 to 280; Leasco from 33⅝ to 139¾; and IBM, the Big Daddy of them all, almost doubled from its year's low of 362½ to a high of 648, an amazing performance for so huge a company, with 54,361,000 shares outstanding.

There is good reason to believe that the better-managed computer and computer-related companies will continue to outperform most other classes of equities for some time to come. Selection of computer securities for gain must be made with care, however, since many issues have advanced spectacularly and some, even after the shakedown in early 1968, are selling at alpine price/ earnings ratios. There must be valid prospects for a continued and sizable gain in future earning power to justify high market prices or to offer legitimate hopes for substantial future advances. In this industry as in any other, in the long run, "Stock prices are the slaves of earning power!"

THE COMPUTER ITSELF

The basic unit in this seething industry is an amazing electronic device called a digital computer. It is the lineal descendant of the abacus, the adding machine, and the comptometer; and it is revolutionizing our lives.

HOW IT WORKS

The digital computer has five essential elements. There are: (1) the input unit, which receives all information fed to the computer; (2) the memory unit, which sorts and stores it; (3) the control unit, which can recall it and send it along on signal for processing; (4) the arithmetic unit, which does the calculations required; and (5) the output unit, which translates electrical signals into sounds or printing that can be understood and/or interpreted by operators. To convert information into a form the computer can accept for processing, a code is used. The most common one is called a binary code, in which all letters or numbers are represented by either 0 or 1. Communication within the computer is achieved by a continuous series of electric pulses. In the total process, words and/or numbers are put in at one end, converted into computer code, and propelled to the proper units in the console for storage, processing, or calculation as required. Then, as ordered by an electric signal, the processed data can be restored to words or numbers and fed out at the terminal end.

APPLICATIONS

The applications of this electronic marvel are legion. Computers can perform in seconds calculations that would require months for an expert mathematician using traditional methods. A computer can recall instantly any item stored in its memory unit. This is a great advance for library technology. For example, a lawyer, instead of poring for days over lawbooks for case references, may be able to receive the required citations in a few moments. The infinite mathematical calculations needed for our space and moon shots would be impossible without computers.

In matters affecting our daily lives, computers are most widely used in the processing of data for business, industry, and finance. Payrolls, accounts receivable and payable, recording of inventory and sales, performance of financial and accounting assignments, and other routine business and clerical tasks can all be handled by computers at great savings in time and labor. In banking, computers are used for check processing, posting to accounts, depositors' statements, investment accounting, stock transfer, and registrar services. Insurance companies use computers to speed the handling of premium notices and collections; and for most actuarial and statistical calculations. The government uses computers in the Post Office, Internal Revenue Service, Social Security Administration, Departments of Defense, Agriculture, and Commerce, and in NASA. Railways and airlines use computers for traffic control and reservation handling. Whole industries — paper, oil, chemical, etc. — use computer systems for operation or process controls and a myriad of machines and machine tools are operated, monitored, and remote-controlled by computers. There is, in fact, no field of human endeavor requiring extensive calculation, mass handling of figures and written data, where the computer will not in due course take over. There's even a service for screening matrimonial compatibility in advance by computer. The computer may control dating as well as data processing!

After these brief observations on the ubiquity of the computer and the attractiveness of this industry for long-term investment or gainful speculation, it's time to look at some specific companies.

THE COMPUTER MANUFACTURERS

The Big Daddy of the industry, IBM, accounted for nearly 65 percent of all computer shipments in 1967. After IBM, a rough listing of significant companies in the market would include Honeywell, Sperry Rand, Control Data, General Electric, Burroughs, RCA, National Cash Register, Digital Equipment, Scientific Data Systems, Wang Laboratories, Applied Dynamics, Barry Wright, and a few others. All these companies make computers of varying sizes and capability, and at the end of 1967, there were approximately 45,000 general-purpose digital computers in use.

Technological advance in computers is rapid, and in something less than a decade we are now in the "third generation" (microelectronic) of computers. The first generation used vacuum tubes, as did our earlier radios.

The second generation (solid-state) represented the switch from tubes to transistors. The fourth generation will probably involve lasers, cryogenics, or both. Computers are like air-transport models — their makers hope they can earn a substantial profit on a given model in the few years' time before it becomes obsolete.

So far, most of the computers made have been leased rather than sold. It is for this reason that computer makers require such heavy investments and large capitalizations. They must not only research, develop, market, and service their models, but finance their total cost as well. The first year of a lease to a customer may show a loss when original installation charges are absorbed; but by the fifth year, leases may become highly profitable. In selecting stocks in individual companies, it is quite important to know how they do their accounting of leases, as that can make a great difference in per share net reported among the various companies. Those that absorb the heaviest first year charges will penalize current earnings, but generate significantly higher earnings in future years. There seems to be a trend now to longer leases (seven to ten years), and some companies are increasing their emphasis on outright sales. On January 4, 1968, IBM announced its new Model 25 of the 360 Computer, for sale at $275,000 or monthly lease at $5,330.

PERIPHERAL EQUIPMENT

A computer is not complete in itself but requires a lot of collateral equipment, which many computer makers buy from others. Most of this equipment falls into two categories, input and output. Input items or devices include card punchers, magnetic ink, and optical character readers, tape drives, magnetic data recorders, and optical scanning equipment. For output, the hardware includes printers, plotters, and cathode-ray tubes, magnetic punched tape and punched cards, disc files and disc packs.

Companies that have gained prominence in peripheral equipment include California Computer Products, Data Products, Memorex, Mohawk Data Sciences, Farrington Manufacturing, WEMS, Inc., Electronic Modules (maker of minicircuitry), and Superior Electric (manufacturer of the patented ultra-flexible Slo-Sun computer motor). You might even include Lewis Business Forms.

COMPUTER LEASING

While all the makers of computers will lease them, there has sprung up, within the industry, a swarm of young companies whose entire business is buying computers and releasing them. Curiously, these companies often lease their machines at rates 10 to 20 percent below those offered by the computer manufacturers. This is because lease companies may pay income taxes at lower rates, gain special benefits from investment tax credits, and usually contract for longer leases than do the manufacturers.

LEVERAGED EQUITIES

Part of the reason for the popularity of computer leasing companies is the high leverage created by their capitalization, which to a great degree consists of debt securities. The general practice is to provide for investors a tempting combination of convertible bonds and warrants together with common stock. New companies have been able to raise their capital easily, and lending institutions find loans to computer leasing companies desirable because the long-term lessors are usually companies of top credit rating, and computers are readily salable assets. Revenues of lease companies can be quite accurately projected for four or five years ahead, and thus capacity to repay indebtedness can be clearly defined.

The factors determining the success of computer leasing companies are (1) management, (2) availability of debt money at reasonable rates, (3) length of leases, and (4) hopefully a long, useful life for each computer model before it is made obsolete by rapid technological advances. Leases in general run between five and ten years. Some lease companies offer programming and professional services in addition.

So far, lease companies have prospered, and most have reported outstanding increases in year-to-year sales and net earnings; and stocks have responded to these gains with great market vigor — as you will note among 1967 market doublers.

This is an easy business field to enter, and as more companies move in, competition will increase. Also, manufacturers may narrow the profit margins of third party lessors by rental reductions of their own, and by making outright purchase more attractive.

Noteworthy companies in leasing include Data Processing Financial and General, Leasco Data Processing, Levin-Townsend, G C Computer, Management Assistance, Granite, Randolph Computer, and Standard Computers. There can be no doubt about the popularity of computer leasing shares, and they exuded capital gains in 1967. The years 1968-69 will test them, and we must beware lest they fall out of market fashion and languish, as did electronic issues in 1962.

SERVICE AND SOFTWARE COMPANIES

The computer business is divided into two major sectors: (1) hardware, which includes all the physical parts and equipment built into computer systems, and (2) software, covering the broad area of instruction in systems analysis and programming, and special services.

Because computers are such sophisticated machines, they require highly trained people to operate them and to carry out the myriad programs assigned to them. Most of these programs involve an input work flow, the translation to computer codes for each program, the computation process, and numerical readouts as end products. The major computer companies go in heavily for training personnel, and a number of independent specialized training schools have also sprung up, some of which have "gone public."

The demand for trained computer personnel is insistent and nationwide, and although there are probably 210,000 qualified operators today, thousands of new trainees are needed. Task assignments are varied and complex, running from rather routine payroll processing to complicated programs required by government, research institutions, space technology, etc. Meeting these personnel demands is a major function of software companies.

Not all customers are big enough to use the full-time services of a computer and staff, so software companies have developed time-sharing plans. Under these, a client with limited computer needs can rent the services of a computer for a period of time, or for the performance of specific programs and tasks. Thousands of companies and organizations fall into this part-time category and represent a rich field for expansion. The computer time can be purchased either (1) from manufacturers, (2) from owners whose equipment is not used all the time or to capacity (possibly a bank or insurance company), or (3) from software companies majoring in the sale of computer time. This time sharing may become a very broad section of the industry, bringing the skills and cost savings of computer systems to very small firms that could never afford to purchase and operate equipment of their own.

There are many small software companies with shares publicly held. Some of the larger and better known ones include Computer Applications, Computing & Software, Computer Sciences.

COMPUTER STOCKS FOR DOUBLING

While many computer shares have doubled and more since issuance, it certainly does not appear that the possibilities for speculative gain in this field are at an end, although a lot more analysis and judgment are now required. Stock prices will follow earning power in this investing field as in any other. There are two main appraisal problems: (1) how rapidly are earnings growing? (2) what is a safe multiple to use for share-price evaluation of these earnings? It would also seem wise to use the "package" approach to speculation here by picking out three or four computer stocks rather than risk all on a single one. We would look for companies whose net earnings are growing at the rate of at least 30 percent annually, and we would hope to buy those earnings at a multiple of 30 or less. In computers, you can't escape paying a premium for growth potentials, market velocity, and glamour. As long as computer issues remain in high market fashion among both individuals and institutions, they will probably continue to do well (and, on occasion, double) if for no other reason than that demand appears greater than market supply.

As specific issues for possible doubling in a year, we would suggest your gathering the latest information about the following: Leasco, Barry Wright, Applied Dynamics, Data Processing Financial and General, Control Data, University Computing, and possibly Burroughs.

5

conglomerates

A major market phenomenon of the past five years has been the emergence and popularity of corporate conglomerates. These are the lineal descendants of the great trusts that waxed strong between 1890 and 1905, except that the trusts were amalgamations of companies all in one industry—the Standard Oil Trust, the American Tobacco Trust, etc. And those, as you will recall, were broken up because they were virtual monopolies.

ANTITRUST POLICEMEN

Government antitrust surveillance and legal action is still a vital factor in any merger being planned today—

witness the ordered divestment in 1967 of three fire sprinkler and alarm companies previously owned by Grinnell Corporation, and the legal roadblocks that derailed the planned merger of International Telephone & Telegraph and American Broadcasting Corporation.

It is apparent that any proposed take-over that may give the emerging company too large a slice of its market will never take place. For example, it would be unthinkable for General Motors, which now has roughly 54 percent of the motorcar market, or for IBM, with 65 percent of the computer market, to acquire another company in their industries.

So it is that the great vertical and horizontal trusts of yore have joined the dodo and the dinosaur in the limbo of history. Big mergers, however, are still with us and in 1967 there were about 2,900 acquisitions completed; and the big ones were all into conglomerates!

WHAT IS A CONGLOMERATE?

A conglomerate is a multiple company created through acquisition or amalgamation of a series of companies in unrelated businesses, and generally operated as semi-independent divisions within the corporate whole. The conglomerate is based on the theory that a talented top-management team including specialists in law, accounting, finance, marketing, research, administration, etc., and generalists (overall coordinators) can maximize the combined profitability of the constituent divisional units. Further, because the conglomerates are, or grow, very large (there are several billion-dollar ones, Textron, Litton, Ling-Temco-Vought, Gulf & Western, etc.), they usually enjoy top credit ratings. They can borrow money in large amounts and at prime rates to finance acquisitions or make "tender" offers. Because of their resources, prestige, and the market popularity of their securities, they have been able, with ease, to make new acquisitions by offering their own common or convertible preferred stock for the equity in exchange.

THE WHOLE IS GREATER THAN THE PARTS

What really occurs here is that the whole, by the magic of the market, becomes greater, often far greater, than the sum of its parts! To illustrate, George J. Meyer Manufacturing Company of Milwaukee was acquired in 1967 by Automatic Sprinkler Corporation, which offered a share-for-share exchange of its stock for Meyer Manufacturing common. Three weeks before the merger offer, Meyer common had sold as low as 28. At the time of the merger negotiations' announcement, Automatic Sprinkler common was selling around 54; and a few weeks later at 71! Thus, simply by moving from an independent company status to a conglomerate one, Meyer Manufacturing rewarded its stockholders with over 100 percent capital gain within two months! It is safe to conclude that Meyer common with earnings of around $2.60 a share would not, by itself, have sold above $50 in 1967 or 1968.

The real reasons for the success of these conglomerates are the market romance they exude, and the speculative followings they generate. Conglomerates make news, with their rumors of negotiation or tender for this or that company making the financial pages with great frequency. Moreover, these companies are fortune builders. Early buyers and patient holders of Litton, Ling, or Teledyne have scored market profits of 2,000 percent or more.

Republic Corporation, formerly a motion picture maker but now a rising conglomerate, generated a market rise in its common from 4½ to 74¼ in 1967, and Ling-Temco-Vought went from a low of 50¼ to a high of 125. Thus, in our quest for stocks that can double in a year, we should certainly plan to include a few conglomerates. Conglomerates, tempered by their sell-off in February, 1968, remain in high market fashion, even though they appear to sell for more than they're really worth. They regularly sell at high price/earnings multiples and can thus buy acquired book value assets by offering "Chinese money," an exchange of stock in one company for stock in another. They have another virtue, too — instant diversification. In a single stock, you can often get representation in a series of rapidly growing industries. The old theory of diversification was to insure against serious erosion or total loss of invested funds by spreading the investment over several issues — defensive diversification. The conglomerates view this matter differently; they're more geared to aggressive diversification, spreading their operation over corporate units selected with potentials for performance in each industrial sector. Many of them have proved their point.

To demonstrate how conglomerates work, we have selected for swift review one of the best of them, Ling-Temco-Vought, a brilliant performer in 1967 and the lengthened shadow of an imaginative corporate leader, James J. Ling, its chairman.

In 1967, Ling made two major moves: it acquired Wilson & Company, with $196 million in assets, and Greatamerica, with $500 million. Ling's operations, unlike those of most conglomerates, are an open book, since all of its operating units are public companies, and not wholly owned subsidiaries, with earnings hidden in consolidated earnings statements. Thus a realistic appraisal of the total worth of LTV may be arrived at by calculating the market value of the shares it owns in these publicly traded subsidiary stocks. Here's a rough listing of the LTV corporate family:

COMPANY	LTV EQUITY OWNERSHIP %	INDUSTRIAL FIELD
LTV Aerospace	74.2	Aircraft and missiles
LTV Electrosystems	67.7	Radio/radar, navigation and guidance systems
LTV Ling Altec	86.1	Hi-fi sound systems, radio and telephone equipment
Okonite	81.7	Power, telephone, control cables
Wilson & Company	75.0	Meat packing, dairy products
Wilson Sporting Goods	66.7	Athletic equipment
Wilson Pharmaceutical & Chemical	69.6	Organic chemicals, resins, pharmaceuticals
Greatamerica		Banks, insurance companies and 80.9% of Braniff Airways, Inc.

LTV is indeed a remarkable company. This broad spread of companies produced sales of some $1.7 billion in 1967 and earned $7 a share on 3,819,000 shares outstanding — a return of about 15 percent on corporate net worth. Investors and speculators who have invested or speculated in LTV common, and its subsidiaries, have done well. Due to the existence of convertible issues, about 2,165,326 shares may be added to outstanding LTV common (as of January 15, 1968), representing a possible dilution of 56 percent. This potential increase in number of common shares will be offset, of course, by the elimination of interest or cash dividends on the senior securities converted; and the proved ability of LTV to generate consistently high returns on its invested capital. LTV common more than doubled in value in 1967. It might even repeat in 1968-69.

In a later chapter, we will outline some specific conglomerates that give promise of above-average market performance and hopeful doubling in a year. Meanwhile, you might like to go over the random selection of representative conglomerates given below, with 1967 additions.

Avco — added Paul Revere Insurance.

Northwest Industries, Inc., formerly *Chicago & Northwestern* — a railway with chemical companies, which recently acquired a full-scale conglomerate, Philadelphia & Reading.

City Investing.

FMC — acquired Link Belt.

General Tire & Rubber.

Gulf & Western — added $325 million in assets: E. W. Bliss, Consolidated Cigar, Universal American.

International Telephone & Telegraph — Sheraton, Leavitt & Sons, Rayonier added.

Kaiser Industries.

Litton — acquired American Book, Landis Tool, Stouffer Foods.

LTV — previously discussed.

Martin Marietta.

National Distillers.

Ogden Corporation.

Olin-Mathieson.

Signal Oil & Gas — added Mack Truck.

Singer Company.

Teledyne.

Tenneco — added Kern County Land.

Textron — a cluster of small companies.

TRW — added United Carr Fastener.

Other conglomerates would include Glen Alden, Walter Kidde & Company, Standard International, and a relative newcomer, National Industries. You might also include in this category American Research & Development, which brought from infancy to great success Digital Equipment, Allied Dynamics, Ionics, etc.

Now, not all conglomerates are outstanding successes. Some pay too dearly for their acquisition, some lack managerial skills in depth, and some take over companies that would have done far better if they had stayed where they were. Therefore, speculators seeking stocks that can double in a year have to screen their conglomerate selections with great care or they may win a hodgepodge package of ill-assorted enterprises with no capacity to increase earnings. To be a winner, a conglomerate must display financial acumen, have cost-conscious innovative management, assemble companies that can be compatibly assimilated. Finally, the conglomerate should be able to increase net earnings 20 percent or more annually to put the right drive in back of its shares. Check this growth rate with great care in the shares you look at.

Caution should also be exercised in 1968-69 not to get into a conglomerate with too heavy a military orientation. Avco, Litton, and Martin Marietta historically have been rather heavy on government business and in their recent acquisitions appear to have been striving to achieve a better balance.

Conglomerates can be annual doublers, and the good ones seem to be insatiable in their urge to merge. Keep combing this field for smartly managed ones with good track records.

6

potential swift profits in new issues

Human beings have always been attracted and excited by novelty. We acclaim and acquire the latest in fashions, motorcars, resorts, the newest books, plays, music, and art forms. We're generally more than willing to pay a premium for this newness. That is just as true in the stock market as anywhere else on this planet. The launching of an exciting new issue in Wall Street has all the glamour of an opening night at the theater, and when OTC trading begins, you know almost instantly whether or not you have a hit on your hands. In the case of a hot newcomer, a third of the issue may be traded in a frantic market on opening day. Those disappointed with allotments received will try to "round them out"; others will enter the trading market for a short swing, and real pros may sell the issue short, if it becomes too gaudily overpriced. For example, when Applied Dynamics (a maker of analogue computers) came out at $12 on December 27, 1967, the stock soared shortly to 39 bid. One shrewd trader sold 1,000 shares at that level and repurchased within ten days at 28. So, for market action and stocks that can not only double in a year but sometimes in a single day, you should be alert to coming new issues. They can be both zestful and rewarding.

1967 — A GOLDEN YEAR FOR NEWCOMERS

In 1967, over $1 billion in new equities were brought to market. Many of these were additional issues of shares of established and well-known companies. Dozens of them, however, were issues of companies presenting, for the first time, an opportunity for investors to become partners in corporations relatively new in business and frequently without any record of operating profits — but plenty of high hopes! All of these were offered by a legal document called a prospectus, unblessed but not disapproved by the Securities and Exchange Commission. This prospectus is a dreary array of legal language, corporate history and projections, description of the financial structure, listing of officers, directors, principal stockholders, and a balance sheet and earnings (if any) statement. It is improbable that any investor or speculator ever read a prospectus through from cover to cover; yet this arid document must legally be presented to each buyer in advance of his purchase to inform him properly of the risks he may be taking. Prospectuses are great, however, for lawyers, who will charge $10,000 or more for a Blackstone Beauty of a prospectus, and the printing, depending on number of copies ordered, will cost from $5,000 up. The prospectus is to a new issue what a program is to a Broadway opening.

THE 1967 MODELS

Approximately 162 new issues were publicly underwritten in 1967. This was by no means an all-time high. In 1961, over 500 new share issues were introduced. But whereas in 1961 there was a spate of small issues, many offered at $3 or below, 1967 marked the entry to public ownership of a substantial number of old, well-established industrial companies with long records of earnings. Many of these qualified for Exchange listing, after a brief apprenticeship in the OTC market. The above figures do not include "Regulation A" issues (of $300,000 or less), which totaled 38 in 1967 against 329 in 1961.

In addition to the shares of many long-established companies offered first in 1967, there were dozens of issues of companies in the newer economic sectors — offshore drilling, nursing homes, air and water pollution control, space age and scientific companies, exotic metals and computers galore. Most of these security emanations of 1967 were both interesting and rewarding.

Volume of trading in new offerings was at an all-time high, and the size and quality of issues was a great improvement over the typical 1961 offering. Of the 162 offerings, the average size was 230,000 shares and the average price about $12. The amazing thing is that about 85 percent of all new offerings in 1967 sold at immediate premiums, and even at the end of the year, four out of five vintage 1967 new issues were selling at higher than subscription prices. Never had so many stocks made such sizable early gains for so many people. It was almost impossible to buy a "turkey."

To appreciate the buoyancy of this new-issue market, and the money people made from confirmed original subscriptions, just look at the list below of standout performers selected at random:

ISSUE	OFFERING DATE		BID PRICE 12/29/67
Aits	May 3	10	36 1/2
Applied Dynamics	Dec. 27	12	31
Applied Magnetics	Aug. 31	15 1/4	38
Cognitronics	Nov. 5	11	34 3/4
Cordis	Oct. 10	55	152
Eberline Instrument	Mar. 29	2.67 (3 for	24 1/2
Graphic Sciences	Sept. 12	10 1)	38
Key Pharmaceuticals	Feb. 27	6 1/2	13 1/2
Lum's	Mar. 22	6.33 (3 for	43
Optics Technology	Aug. 10	12 1)	43 1/2
Safeguard Industries	June 14	10	34
Wadell Equipment	Oct. 12	9 1/2	23
Wang Laboratories	Aug. 23	12 1/2	66

The lure of new companies, exciting technologies, rising sales, and small capitalizations was all that was needed to double or treble many share prices, long before the six-month holding period was over.

Because of the potential profits to be derived from shrewd or fortunate original subscriptions to new issues, it is important that you keep on the lookout for them. How do you do this? By reading the daily financial pages and certain weekly financial journals which list proposed new issues and those already in registration. (Securities may remain in registration from two to several months.) *The Commercial and Financial Chronicle* (which carries my feature article each week) has in its Monday edition and in its *O-T-C Market Chronicle* (which comes out twice a month) a section headed "Securities Now in Registration." *Investment Dealers' Digest* also publishes a list of securities in registration. These lists usually recite the company in registration, the amount of the financing, and the name of the principal underwriter. With this information, you can contact the underwriter and request a prospectus, when ready. You may even write to the company itself to order its latest balance sheet, a catalogue of its products, or any other information about its operations that it will supply.

If you're really interested in a new issue, you should endeavor to find out all you can about it. Learn what the company does, its reputation for leadership or pioneer research in its field, who its competitors and customers are and how they view the company.

After you have made sufficient inquiry and possibly received a "red herring" (an advance copy of the prospectus that does not give the offering price), you may decide to subscribe. The best way to do this is to contact the head underwriting firm or a member of the syndicate or selling group offering the stock. Many firms do not make available shares in attractive new issues to any but their own steady customers; so you may want to open an account in advance with the brokerage firm that will offer the particular shares you seek. You may also want to place several orders with different houses, or perhaps subscribe through your bank to secure a satisfactory subscription allotment. Don't be a pig when subscribing. Order 100 to 300 shares (not 1,000) at any one place. If you are genuinely convinced about the early potentials of this issue, then you may even want to pay a premium price in the OTC market in order to have a position in it. As an avid trader seeking to double your money, you may later follow "operation baitback," that is, sell half of your stock once it has doubled in price.

WHAT MAKES A "HOT" ISSUE?

Naturally, in subscribing to new issues in quest of swift capital gain, you will hope to develop some way of selecting and screening issues most likely to go up swiftly and substantially. Is there any way to do this? Yes, there is. There are certain criteria to look for. New issues as well as seasoned stocks that double have certain special qualities.

First of all, the industry in which the company does business should be one currently popular and "fashionable" among speculators. In 1967, such industries were computers, producing oil companies, hamburgers, silver, scientific research, hydraulics, miniature and modular electronic circuitry, and motels. Each year there is an "in" group of industries, and speculative success is more likely to result if you confine new issue purchases to those industries.

Secondly, look for small capitalization. It is quite common for corporations "going public" to offer 30 to 40 percent of their equity in an underwriting, with 60 to 70 percent retained by original or management group. For example, a company with 750,000 shares of common, authorized and to be outstanding, may offer 250,000 shares to the public at $10 a share. That's $2.5 million in total new money. If only 2,500 people buy 100 shares each, the stock will be fully subscribed for. What happens, however, in the case of a typical glamorous and well-heralded issue, is that 5,000 people may enter subscriptions averaging 200 shares each, so that subscriptions received may aggregate $10 million, and the issue be four times oversubscribed. Because of the demand-supply relationship thus set. up, the issue in question is almost certain to advance to a substantial premium due to scarcity alone and without any reference to the intrinsic merits of the offering. So seck not only issues with a favorable conjecture but those with a relatively small "floating supply."

Third, stress management. Among new computer

company issues, those that have performed best are headed by men usually successful and well trained for leadership by virtue of earlier affiliation with the leaders in the industry. In scientific equities, management should be especially strong in two areas: technology and re- search, and sales. In motels, financial skill topside, a shrewdness in site selection, and effective unit managers are the vital management ingredients; in advertising, creative and innovative talents are indispensable to suc- cess. In any company, seek management that is young, aggressive, well trained in its field, profit-hungry, and stock-owning.

Fourth, check up on the underwriting record of the firm or firms that are sponsoring the issue. Certain Wall Street houses have had outstanding success in presenting new offerings that "go out the window." Get on the subscrip- tion lists of those houses!

Finally, subscribe to newcomers only when a bull mar- ket is roaring. New issues even of top quality and great promise can lay an egg if the market is going down. The time to double your money in either new or old issues is in bull market years. Nineteen sixty-seven was such!

We'd like to offer some specific suggestions about the new issues you may buy that can possibly double (and bring happiness) in a year, but we haven't a crystal ball for naming them in advance. For 1968-69, we can only offer background guidelines to those industries that give promise of being in high market fashion. We believe these will include medical centers and nursing homes; leisure time and adult education (like Famous Artists Schools); Canadian and offshore oil drilling; gold, nickel, and as- bestos; publishing; mutual funds and life insurance com- bined; oceanography and professional football. Look for new companies and new issues in these industrial sectors and you may be in the mainstream of fashion- able stocks for growth and gain — if we're in a bull market.

7

speculation in investment-company shares

Most speculation, whether in shares purchased for long-term gain or for doubling and selling within a year, is confined to issues of individual corporations — Polaroid, Control Data, Occidental Petroleum, Kentucky Fried Chicken, Litton, Cubic Corporation for example. But there is considerable interest today in the speculative possibilities of mutual funds and investment companies.

Investment companies (or investment trusts, as they are sometimes called) first appeared in the United States in the 1920's. They were modeled after British and Scottish investment trusts, which had done well by investors for many years.

Investment companies or investment trusts were created to assemble and pool together the contributions of capital from many individuals and to invest these funds prudently in diversified marketable securities for safety, income, and possible long-term gains. The basic idea was to provide for those not informed, interested, or skilled in investment matters continuous professional security management. In addition, investment-company shares were designed to provide safe custody of securities, sound judgment in security purchase and sales, proper timing thereof, and broad diversification to insulate portfolios from excessive loss due to the failure of any single security or company. Investment companies caught on rapidly in 1927-29. Unfortunately, most of the securities bought for investment-company portfolios, particularly common stocks, were (1) acquired at the very high prices then prevailing and (2) on occasion sold to a trust or fund by a banking house that sought to "lay off" or dispose of an issue of either dubious merit or market acceptability. Two or three of these trusts proved to be dumping grounds for indigestible and hazardous securities. Quite naturally these performed miserably and sank to dismal lows during the Great Depression.

MODERN INVESTMENT COMPANIES

Those days, however, are all behind us and, with the arrival on the scene of the Securities and Exchange Commission and the Investment Company Act of 1940, investment-company business has been effectively regulated and has brought investment success and serenity to millions. Today there are over 300 domestic mutual funds, and investment companies with total assets of over $45 billion.

There are actually two main types of investment company: (1) the open-end or mutual fund, and (2) the closed-end investment company.

Mutual funds — far more popular, with over 4 million shareholders — are investment companies wherein individuals, corporations, or trusts buy shares and thus supply capital invested and managed by professionally trained investment counsel, for a fee. This fee may be ½ of 1 percent annually on the total value of the portfolio, or it may be a little less if the trust or fund is very large. On any business day a mutual fund may sell its shares to investors; and on the same day may redeem (buy in) its shares from prior owners at net prices. These net prices are the actual calculated total market value of all the securities then in the trust portfolio divided by the total number of shares outstanding. Generally, at the time of purchase, funds make a charge of a certain amount per share. This sales charge, or load, may be as high as 8½ percent, and its purpose is to defray costs of advertising and promoting the fund and payment of commissions to salesmen. It is also a "round trip" charge, since customarily no charge is made if or when the shareholder redeems (sells) his shares. Some funds sell their shares at net prices without any sales commission charged. In either case, there is customarily a separate management company which handles promotion and sale of shares, supervises the portfolio, and makes the market decisions to buy, sell, or hold specific securities. Mutual funds have (usually) but one class of stock, and the number of their shares outstanding varies from day to day (which is why they are called open-end funds).

CLOSED-END COMPANIES

The second class of investment trust is called closed-end because the number of its shares outstanding does not vary from day to day; and is not increased except by a stock dividend or special corporate authorization to enlarge the capitalization. Thus investors wishing to buy purchase shares in closed-end investment companies must buy them from parties who already own the shares. Closed-end investment companies have active daily trading markets and most are listed on major exchanges. Tri-Continental, Atlas Corporation, Alleghany Corporation, Adams Express, Lehman Corporation, Dominick Fund, Madison Fund, Electric Bond & Share are examples of closed-end funds. All have extensive, and usually widely diversified, portfolios, all trade actively, and some are leveraged by the existence of debentures or preferred stock senior to the common stocks in the capital structures. Another distinguishing feature of closed-end companies is that they are managed by their own board of directors instead of by a separate management company. These directors elect the salaried officers who actually administer and manage the portfolios. There is no management fee charged and, in purchasing or selling closed-end company shares, the investor is charged a regular stock exchange commission. Whereas most mutual funds' asset values and offering prices are quoted in metropolitan daily papers, closed-end shares are bought and sold by market auction, and share prices may vary from one transaction to the next as supply and demand factors in the issue may dictate. As a matter of fact, many closed-end company shares sell at sizable discounts from their net asset value, the discount depending usually on the reputation of management and its historic record for investment success (or lack of it).

BALANCED AND SPECIAL-PURPOSE FUNDS

At the start, investment companies of both kinds sought to be general or balanced funds; that is, they acquired broad and diversified lists of frequently sizable percentages in bonds or preferred stocks. Their purpose was to consolidate into a single investment vehicle — in a single share of stock — a complete investment program combining income, safety, marketability, and growth potential. As trusts grew in popular acceptance, funds for special purposes were introduced and grew rapidly: income funds for those seeking good current yields, bond funds, growth funds where dividend income is deliberately sacrificed to maximize capital gain, and funds concentrating in particular industries, such as Energy Fund, Television and Electronics Fund, Value Line Special Situation Fund, Capital Shares and Life Insurance Investors, specializing in insurance stocks, Chemical Fund, and, most recently, Oceanography Fund.

PERFORMANCE FUNDS

For years it was the custom of most fund managements to confine purchases to seasoned blue chip stocks of great corporations, and to retain issues quite indefinitely. Decision to sell securities was usually made in individual issues for valid and fundamental reasons (decline in earnings, poor management, a deteriorating industry, cyclical characteristics); or to exchange one security for a better or more undervalued one in the same industry or price range. Many trusts, both closed-ends and mutuals, still adhere to this conservative policy. These would include Investors Mutual and Wellington Fund among open-ends, and Adams Express and Tri-Continental among closed-ends. These conservatively managed trusts, while preserving good levels of dividend income, may not produce significant or impressive gains in value from year to year. Trusts of this broadly diversified kind (and there are several very large ones) make no logical appeal to speculators seeking to double their money within a single year.

There is, however, a new theory of fund management that has gained great acceptance in the past five years. This theory calls for active trading of fund portfolios and concentrating investments in those industries and companies holding promise of swift capital gains. Such time-honored qualities as book values, dividends, current assets are quite ignored in such funds. Instead, purchases are made based principally on growth in earnings, not in the past or currently so much as in the year or years ahead. Whereas, as this was written, the Dow-Jones Industrial stocks were selling at 16.5 times earnings, investment managers were willing to pay 40 or 50 times earnings for shares in companies growing five times as fast as the economy and promising to continue to do so in coming years. These "hot" stocks often sell on an optimistic projection of earnings four years ahead. Thus, especially in 1967-68, managers of many trusts gave relatively slight attention to such "traditionals" as U.S. Steel, Anaconda Copper, International Paper, General Foods, and General Electric, but were eager to acquire Famous Artists Schools, Kentucky Fried Chicken, Control Data, EG&G, Wang Laboratories, Kerr-McGee, and Data Processing Financial and General at gaudy earnings multiples. Computer, instrument, service, or science companies have become market favorites.

This stress on performance and market velocity rather than on investment fundamentals has glamorized a whole new generation of investment managers. Young men like Gerald Tsai at Manhattan Fund and Cal Hathaway, head shepherd of institutional investment at Morgan Guaranty Trust Company, are examples of this new breed. The traditional investment committee composed of steely-eyed, gray-headed elder financier and trustee types has been replaced by smaller teams of portfolio managers or even one-man marketeers, all below age forty. In the roaring market year of 1967, the "go-go" approach to portfolio management was prevalent not only in investment companies but in pension and endowment funds as well. Many of these funds performed spectacularly. Some were so active in their trading that they turned over 50 percent of their entire portfolio assets within the year.

Representative closed-end performance in 1967 is illustrated by the following gains in representative issues.

APPROXIMATE 1967 GAINS IN ASSET VALUE

(Including dividends received, market appreciation, and realized gains)

	% GAINED
Madison Fund	42
Dominick Fund	32.9
Adams Express	28.5
Lehman	27.6
General American Investors	27.1
Tri-Continental	25.1
American International	25

Mutual funds generally, and especially those stressing "performance" goals, outperformed the "closed-ends" in 1967. While the Dow-Jones Industrial Average rose in 1967 by 15.2 percent, the average rise in per share value (market appreciation plus realized gains) of over 150 substantial mutual funds was approximately 27 percent. A number of the mutuals did much better than that, as evidenced by the following results of certain outstanding performers selected at random:

YEAR 1967

FUND	% GAIN IN PER SHARE VALUE
Enterprise Fund	113.9
Value Line Special Situations	99.8
Rowe Price New Horizons	95.3
Axe Science	83.5
Chase Fund	79.4
B. C. Morton Growth	76.2
Keystone S4	62
Pilgrim Fund	60

(None of these funds gained even as much as 10 percent in dreary 1966.)

This is but a partial list, selected only to illustrate the size of gains attainable where managements drive hard — and in many cases take sizable risks — to achieve stand-out performance. The list proves also that it is possible even in broadly diversified funds to find happiness in a stock that doubles in a year.

INVESTMENT COMPANIES DESIGNED FOR THE SPECULATOR

There are two new types of investment companies that have recently entered the field and are designed specifically for the speculatively minded.

Dual-Purpose Funds. The first is the dual-purpose fund. This investment trust seeks to meet two major investment objectives by splitting its shares into two categories: Income Shares and Capital Shares.

To illustrate the "split" or dual fund, we offer a hypothetical example. The Serenity Dual Fund (a closed-end trust) is created with $20 million in original paid-in capital. Under the dual-purpose formula, this capital would be divided into two sections: $10 million in Income Shares offered at $10, each entitled to 60 cents minimum in cumulative annual dividends, payable out of net income; and $10 million in Capital Shares, entitled to receive all capital appreciation.

The Income Shares at $10 are entitled to all the net income of the trust. Operating expenses (excluding brokerage commissions and transfer taxes, which are part of the cost of securities) are borne by Income Shareholders. Then, at the end of fifteen years, these Income Shares are scheduled for redemption at $10; and all the assets of the trust remaining after this redemption will belong to Capital Shareholders. The Income Shareholders may, however, be given the privilege, at that time, of converting their shares (instead of redeeming them) into Capital Shares, applying the $10 redemption price against Capital Shares acquired at their (then) asset value. *The important element in both issues is their 2 to 1 initial leverage. The $10 million invested in Income Shares gets all the net income* not from $10 million but from $20 million, by forgoing any share in capital gains. The Capital Shares in turn will receive substantially *no dividends or distributions, but receive or accrue all capital gains and after fifteen years be entitled to receive all net income* as well as accumulated and future gains of the company. Here again there's a 2 to 1 leverage at work. The $10 million in Capital Shares gets all the market appreciation on the original $20 million. It is this 2 to 1 leverage, working uniquely for both classes of stock, that makes these funds so intriguing.

PROJECTIONS

To define the special advantages of these trusts, we shall present some hypothetical returns on each class of stock. In projecting our estimates, we have made two reasonable assumptions: (1) that an averaged annual income return of at least 3½ percent is expectable on the total portfolio, and (2) that averaged market appreciation of at least 3½ percent annually should be realized. (These assumptions are indeed conservative, since the actual results of a whole series of pension and endowment funds, employing common stocks, were substantially above 3½ percent per annum in both categories over the past forty years.)

Observe what a minimum 3½ percent return can do for the Income stock of Serenity Fund. A 3½ percent return on $20 million is $700,000 annually, or 7 percent on each $10 Income Share. This income (and the percentage thereof) may be increased substantially, however, during the fifteen years for two reasons:

1. Growth-type stocks, presumably selected, are notable for their steady dividend increases. Issues such as IBM, McGraw-Hill, Sears, Roebuck, American Hospital Supply, American Home Products, Ametek, American Electric Power, have all increased their dividends at least six times in the past decade.

2. As capital gains are realized, the total invested funds will be correspondingly increased, and the assumed 3½ percent minimum will, hopefully, apply not to $20 million but to a steadily larger principal amount. It is quite possible to envision an annual return to Income Shareholders of as much as 12 percent, on original investment, during later years. These Income Shares are really a participating preferred stock and might far outperform, over the years, fixed-return high-grade bonds and preferred issues customarily employed for income purposes.

How will the Capital Shareholder fare under this dual formula? He gives up all income, but look what he gets: the capital gains on not $10 million but $20 million (plus). Using the 3½ percent gain figure, this equals 7 percent on each share annually, or a total of $10.50 per share in fifteen years. This would suggest that Capital Shares costing $10 should, at a minimum and without compounding, be worth at least $20.50 at the end of fifteen years. With sophisticated management of an equity portfolio, an average annual gain in asset value of 5 percent compounded is entirely possible. Using the 2 to 1 leverage, this compounded rate of gain would make Capital Shares worth around $30 in fifteen years and the shares would then be in line to receive *all income* from the fund as well (after Income Share redemption).

The prospectuses, of course, do not (and could not) allude to any such gain potentials as we have projected in respect to either income or gain; but some of the men who have organized these dual funds would not regard these growth estimates as particularly optimistic. It is also obvious that a 50 percent decline in original asset value would give the Capital Shares an asset value of zero or less!

These dual funds are all closed-end, and most of them are listed on the New York Stock Exchange. Here's a partial list of some of the major "duals":

> American Dualvest
> Gemini
> Hemisphere
> Income & Capital
> Putnam Duo Fund
> Scudder Duo-Vest

It is apparent that the 2 to 1 leverage factor is very important here and that speculation in the Capital Shares of well-managed "duals" in a bull-market year could be most rewarding. Doubling your money here in a year is a possibility, however remote.

HEDGE FUNDS

The latest variety of investment company, with by all means the most exciting speculative potentials, is the hedge fund. This started out as a partnership of individuals who entrusted units of capital — $10,000, $25,000, $50,000, or more — to an investment manager. He set out to create capital gains for these clients or associates (with their consent) by employment of most flexible investment techniques. These techniques might include, in addition to customary investment practices, the use of short sales, put-and-call options, and leverage created through borrowing. Some of these hedge-fund partnerships were outstandingly successful, and in a good market year, such as 1967, it was not uncommon for them to produce market gains of 100 percent or more. As you can imagine, the success depends almost entirely on the wisdom, judgment, experience, and market agility of the manager. He is usually rewarded by an investment-counsel fee of from $\frac{5}{8}$ percent to as much as 20 percent, depending on his skill or the extent to which his portfolio outperforms the Dow-Jones or Standard & Poor's Index.

While many hedge funds are still operated as partnerships, more recently there have come to the market hedge funds publicly underwritten, which are open-end, diversified mutual funds. These do not pretend to be complete or balanced funds, and they make no appeal to individuals whose main objective is dependable income or mere preservation of capital. Hedge funds are for speculators questing for swift capital gains, who are willing to delegate the portfolio management to nimble market operators who usually have established a reputation for adroitness and sureness in trading and the ability to "sell short," as well as to invest rewardingly on the "long" side. You might want to look at Hedge Fund of America, The Hubshman Fund, or others, which may be offered from time to time.

CONCLUSION

We may conclude that conservative, balanced mutual funds or closed-end funds seem unlikely vehicles for swift capital gain. Accordingly, it would be our thought that these funds, however useful as conservative and moderately growing long-term investment, do not meet our purpose.

If 100 percent market gain in a year is to be achieved, we believe that the best place to seek it among investment companies is either in the special-situation or performance-oriented mutuals similar to the group we listed above, or in hedge funds with proved successful managements, and possibly among the most aggressively managed dual funds. In any event, you must remember that anything you read in this chapter is under no circumstance to be regarded as a recommendation, offering, or endorsement of any fund, mutual or otherwise. If you are to speculate in this area, you must acquire, and rely totally on, the prospectus, which according to law must be delivered to the buyer or prospective buyer of a mutual fund prior to his purchase. Neither the "hottest" managed fund nor a group of individual stocks may be expected to advance spectacularly or double in a single year unless the market generally is in a bull-market upsurge. Many investors, however, who have the urge to speculate but lack the required knowledge or skill may get rewarding results by well-timed purchase of a performance-slanted mutual or hedge fund. The hedge fund is unique in the potential for increasing asset values, even in a poor market year, by clever and well-timed short sales.

8

unusual speculative risks and gains in warrants, puts, and calls

The most sensational stock-market gains, on the least dollar outlays, can with good fortune be obtained without ever owning stocks at all! You merely purchase the privilege of buying or selling a share or shares of stock at a certain price within a certain time period.

There are three unique market vehicles that make this kind of speculation possible: warrants, puts, and calls. We'll talk about the warrants first.

WARRANTS — FINANCIAL WILL-O'-THE-WISPS

The ingenuity of financial minds has for years sought techniques for benefiting from the price advance of common stocks with (1) a maximum of gain and (2) a minimum of outlay. One such technique is to buy stocks on borrowed money (on margin), through a responsible broker, or by loan from a bank. The slickest device for the purpose, however, is a tricky security called a stock purchase warrant. A warrant is not a bond or a stock; it never has any book value; it never pays a dividend or shares in profits or losses; it is eternally devoid of any lien or claim on assets or earning power; yet it can, under fortunate circumstances, create the widest imaginable swings in market value. A warrant can deliver gains running into thousands of percent; or it can swiftly become totally worthless.

Essentially a warrant is an agreement or contract on the part of a corporation to sell a share or shares or fractional shares of its common stock to the warrant holder at a specified price and usually for a limited period of time; but sometimes without time limit. A warrant carries a powerful speculative potential because the market value of the warrant will follow, almost automatically, the market action of the related stock. But while the related common stock may gain 100 percent in a given time interval, the warrant will usually gain at a much higher rate.

In speculating in warrants one must consider: (1) the possibility of rise in the correlated common stock; (2) the price one pays for the warrant; and (3) how much time one has before the warrant expires. Warrants are usually most attractive (and cheapest) in the early phases of bull markets. They are seldom worth more than one-third of the market price of the related stock; and they operate in a rather mathematical relationship to a common stock, somewhat like a moon to a planet. They always seem to sell at more than they are worth. They have, moreover, a sort of built-in market value that gives them a market price where no real value exists, and a premium price when actual mathematical value can be established.

Here are a few examples of warrants, selected at random from the market of April 19, 1968:

EXAMPLES OF COMMON STOCK WARRANTS
PRICES AS OF APRIL 19, 1968

ISSUE	OF WARRANT	OF COMMON	EXPIRATION DATE	PROVISION TO BUY
Alleghany	3 1/8	5 1/4	Perpetual	1 share @ $3.75
Atlas	9 3/8	15 1/8	Perpetual	1 share @ $6.25
Ling-Temco-Vought	55	121 1/2		1 share @ $115
Tri-Continental	56	29 1/2	Perpetual	1.27 shares @ $17.76 per share

Note the chronic tendency of warrants to be overpriced. Ling-Temco warrants on the above date were actually worth 6½, yet they sold at 55; Atlas warrants were worth 8¾, yet they sold at 9⅜.

THE USES OF WARRANTS

The earliest warrants were issued in the reorganization of companies in financial difficulties, as compensation for past financial loss or as a sweetener to make new securities, offered in reorganization or financial readjustment, and none too sturdy investment-wise, more attractive. To illustrate, in 1933 Baldwin Locomotive Works had a bond issue coming due and simply did not have available, in that Depression year, the money needed to pay it off. Accordingly, in order to avoid receivership

or bankruptcy, Baldwin offered to the holder of each
$100 bond 40 warrants to buy Baldwin common stock dur-
ing the next five years at $5 a share, if he would accept,
in lieu of cash redemption of his bond, a new five-year
note of the company of the same par amount. The bond-
holders went along with the plan, the company stayed
alive, and within three years Baldwin common sold at
$20, giving the 40 warrants a minimum value of $15 a-
piece or $600 total. Quite a reward for trust in the com-
pany, plus a little patience!

Warrants Issued with Bonds. Often younger, rapidly
growing companies will publicly offer their bonds with
warrants attached. An example of this was the issue of
Western Homestead 6½'s. The bonds were offered for
public subscription at par and carried 100 warrants,
each permitting the holder to buy a share of common at
$3 through 1972.

The advantages to a company in issuing bonds with
warrants are threefold: (1) the bonds will carry a lower
interest rate (than plain bonds or debentures) because
of the warrant feature; (2) the bonds will be easier to
sell and, accordingly, the company will have lower underwriting commissions to pay to its investment bankers;
and (3) the warrants create a built-in program for future
financing of the corporation, since when (and if) the warrant is exercised, new equity funds will automatically
flow into the corporate treasury.

Warrants Issued with Stocks. On occasion, the financing of newer, early-phase corporations may be done by
original public offering of common stock in conjunction
with warrants. For example, Brun Sensors offered by prospectus on 50,000 units consisting of 2 shares of common
and 1 warrant to buy the common at $6. The unit was of-
fered at 11½. By March, 1968, the common was quoted
in the OTC at 6 bid and the warrants at 2½.

Warrants to Investment Bankers. It is fairly common in

the cases of small, relatively new corporations for their investment bankers to be given a certain number of warrants as part compensation for publicly distributing the new issue. Carrying on with the Brun offering mentioned above, the bankers received 10,000 warrants to buy Brun common at $6.

Warrants to Implement Mergers. On occasion, the acquiring company in a merger may offer warrants in addition to other securities — bonds or shares to "sweeten" the deal and better assure the acceptance of the exchange offer by shareholders in the "selling out" company. Ling-Temco-Vought warrants to buy common stock at $115 were issued in connection with LTV's acquisition of Wilson & Company.

The foregoing provides a summary of most of the occasions on which warrants are issued and become, in due course, marketable securities. There are now several hundred issues of warrants on the market, and dozens of new ones become available each year from the sources described above.

In our avowed purpose to seek securities (mostly common stocks) that can double in twelve months, we should certainly be on the lookout for attractive and underpriced warrants. In a good market year, the gains from them can be most rewarding, and warrants tie up far less cash than an outright purchase of the common stock in the same company. Moreover, the leverage in warrants is such that, in a given time period, the warrant may go up twice or three times as fast as the common stock it is tied to. In 1967, for example, Uris Buildings Corporation common advanced from a low of 15¾ to a high of 33½, while the warrant went from 6⅛ to 23½.

You should again be cautioned that while warrants may soar spectacularly in bull markets, they can also sink dismally in bear ones. Warrants illustrate the old adage: "The farther you're out on the dog's tail, the wider the swing!" Later on, we have listed some warrants as having, with luck, some chance of doubling in a year. In any event, warrants are fascinating, volatile, and zestful, and your life will never be dull if you're riding them in the market. One final word: nothing is more dead or worthless than a warrant that has expired!

PUTS AND CALLS

Within the past five years, there has been rising enthusiasm and endorsement by countless thousands of speculators of two quite special security contracts, called puts and calls. These are exciting devices for reaping stock-market profits without trading in stocks. They can also lose money for you at very high speed! Their attraction is magnetic — an opportunity to make a market killing without any actual buying or selling of stock, with only a very small cash outlay, and with your maximum possible total loss defined in advance. Puts and calls are now one of the fastest growing sectors of business in Wall Street.

A *call* (or call option, as it is more accurately defined) gives you the right to buy 100 shares of the stock of a given company during a stated period of time. The periods of option time may run for thirty, sixty, or ninety days, or for six months and even longer; and the price of the option is invariably higher for issues with a history of market volatility and wide swings. The call or "striking" price is most frequently the current market price at the time the option is arranged, although it may be a point or so higher. For this option, the buyer pays a sum of money called a premium. In the case of the standard six-month option, this premium might be 12 to 16 percent of the total cost of 100 shares at current prices; for shorter periods, less.

A *put* is just the opposite. It permits you to sell 100 shares of a specified stock at a price above the current one, again within a specified time period. And again, the premium will usually be between 12 and 16 percent.

The call is the thing to buy if you think a particular stock will advance substantially in the half year ahead; and you buy the put if you think a given stock is swiftly headed for lower prices.

To see how the profits in these options may be made, let's take a hypothetical example.

Assume that you thought on March 1, 1968, that Automatic Sprinkler had a good chance to go up. You might have picked that stock because it had fallen from a 1967 high of 74 to around 33, and you thought the issue offered a good chance to rebound. Accordingly you bought a six-month call on 100 shares at 33, for which you paid $495. It is obvious that to make any money on this deal, AS would have to sell at 38 or above ($3,300 plus $495). Suppose you were right and the stock moved to $50 within the six-month interval. Your gain (less commission) would actually be $1,205, representing the selling price, $5,000, less your cost ($3,300 plus $495, or $3,795). As you can see, this is an excellent return on your $495 and a far higher percentage of gain on your invested capital than if you had put up $3,300 to buy 100 shares of AS at $33 and sold it at $50 for a total pretax gain of $1,700 (on your $3,300). While the gain from the option in this instance was most rewarding, the possible loss was a total one. The stock had to advance 15 percent for you to break even; while if you had owned the stock outright, you might have had a loss in market value but not a total and unrecoverable one. As long as you own a stock, even though it descends dismally, you may wait patiently for a fairer day when it may zoom. But once the option period has passed and the stock has failed to advance as you had hoped, your loss is complete and final. (The mathematics of a put is of course reversed — the subject stock must decline 12 to 15 percent below your "sell" price or you will field a loss.) Actually, many speculators in options never buy or sell the subject stocks but, rather, sell their winning options back to the broker or dealer and thus realize approximately the same market gains without the bother of actual "buy" and "sell" executions.

The equation in calls appears more favorable than in puts, because calls are customarily at or around current market price, whereas puts are written several points above.

Puts and calls are indeed big business in Wall Street today. In 1967, put and call options were written on over 30 million shares. Because Americans are congenital optimists, about 70 percent of all options written are calls and 30 percent puts. Of course, these percentages will vary with market conditions, and in a roaring bull market over 90 percent of the option-writing will be in calls.

Exercise of options is something else again. Over 80 percent of all calls are exercised in bull markets, but less than 30 percent in bear ones. A lower percentage of puts is exercised, probably not above 65 percent even in a soggy bear market. There is very little market interest in writing options on top-grade blue chips such as AT&T, Standard of New Jersey, American Electric Power, General Electric, which move in relatively narrow market ranges and thus offer no great swings necessary for profits from option. When options are written on blue chips, the premium may dip to as low as 5 percent.

ORIGIN OF PUTS AND CALLS

All puts and calls originate with actual holders of given stocks. For example, persons of wealth, and investment institutions, particularly mutual funds, may be willing to write puts and calls against the shares they own. The writer (the stock owner) has a pretty certain profit in the call option. He gets most of the premium (except for the percentage taken by the broker or put-and-call firm). If the stock optioned really takes off, he will miss part of the action, but he will be compensated by the money received from the premium. If the stock does nothing, the owner still has his shares plus the premium he received, and the option buyer is completely out of luck. There's nothing to stop a share owner from writing two to four options a year on the same stock if his luck holds. The put may be very costly to the writer if a steep decline in the price of a stock compels him to accept stock under the option agreement at a price far above the prevailing market. The money the writer received for the put, however, helps to cushion the fall; and if he had merely held his shares without receiving the option money, he would obviously have borne the market loss in full.

In actual practice, in a sizable portfolio where option writing is done extensively, the writers usually come out winners for the reason that in any normal six-month period, only a small percentage of actively traded stocks will vary one way or the other by more than 15 percent. While writers may earn with some consistency net returns of between 10 and 20 percent in a market year, probably less than one option out of three shows a net profit to the buyer. When he wins, however, he may win big; and gains of 200 to 500 percent on the money risked are not uncommon.

There's a combination of puts and calls which we neglected to mention. It's called a *straddle* and for a larger percentage, frequently 20 percent or more, it gives you the privilege of going either way in the market — either buying or selling 100 shares of a stock over a stated period at agreed prices. This is a highly sophisticated contract and is not recommended for amateurs. Actually, it appeals to those who can't really make up their minds which way a stock may go. Obviously if you are convinced that a stock

is going up, you should not be interested in an option permitting you to lay it off at lower prices. Straddles pay off
only in periods of unusually wide market gyrations.

Assuming that you are intrigued by puts and calls as a
low-cost, short-term speculative vehicle for doubling your
money or better, you'll want to know more about them and
where you can buy them. There are about twenty-five
firms in New York that deal regularly in puts and calls,
and a dozen substantial Stock Exchange firms, with many
branch offices, now handle them.

The procedure is for you, the speculator, to decide on
the stock that you believe has a chance to go either up or
down 20 percent or more in the next six months. Having
selected your "target" issue, inquire of a brokerage firm
or put-and-call dealer if he can write an option for you
on that stock. He will then seek, among his customers or
perhaps among financial institutions, persons or firms
who own that stock and will be willing to write an option
on it. When he has located a "writer," he will so report
to you and quote you the premium and the "striking point"
price for the time interval you select. Then presumably
you buy, and wait for Dame Fortune (and the market) to
smile on you. Because of the inherent and high risks in
these options, you may find it best to buy them on several
stocks, hoping to make, on a single winner, enough money
to cover possible losses on the ones that don't come in.

You need not search far to find firms offering puts and
calls. In *The New York Times* and other big metropolitan
dailies, puts and calls are advertised extensively and the
premiums quoted for a whole list of stocks. This may make
unnecessary your searching for a stock likely to move
sharply — some one of the options offered is likely to give
you one you like. Below are a dozen various options selected at random from those listed on March 1, 1968.
They will give you a good idea of the options available,
and the range of premiums on shares of varying volatility.

SIX-MONTH CALL OPTIONS (100 SHARES)

CLOSING	ISSUE	STRIKING PRICE	COST
11 1/2	American Motors	12 1/2	$ 200.00
136	American Research	138	2,150.00
50 3/8	Chrysler	51 1/4	587.50
61 5/8	Fairchild Camera	62 1/2	987.50
20	General Aniline	20 7/8	325.00
30 1/2	Occidental Petroleum	29 7/8	487.50
78 1/4	Raytheon	79	1,150.00
88 5/8	Texas Instruments	90	1,275.00
27 3/4	Western Air Lines	28 1/4	450.00

SIX-MONTH PUT OPTIONS (100 SHARES)

CLOSING	ISSUE	STRIKING PRICE	COST
33	Avnet	37 1/8	675.00
21 1/8	Flying Tiger	22 7/8	325.00
577	IBM	589 1/2	4,250.00
50 1/2	P. R. Mallory	52 1/2	725.00
43 3/4	Monogram Industries	46 1/2	1,175.00
29 7/8	Pan American Sulphur	30	475.00
22 1/2	Ramada Inns	23 3/8	387.50

This chapter on warrants, puts, and calls is of major interest to avid speculators and risk takers. It also points to a way of doubling your money when the market is going down via calls. All of these vehicles — warrants, puts, and calls — are exciting, and with knowledge and luck can make money for you!

9

the big possible swings in convertible bonds and preferred stocks

In an interesting recent book, *Anyone Can Make a Million,* by Morton Shulman, a Canadian coroner who has done well in the security markets, an excellent case was made for speculation in convertible bonds. These are indeed profit prone and potentially rewarding, so we shall devote a full chapter to them and their next of kin, convertible preferreds.

CONVERTIBLE BONDS

Convertible securities are fascinating senior corporate securities. Under certain conditions, they may be exchanged into junior securities, usually common stocks. We'll look at them first from the standpoint of the investor-speculator, and second from that of the issuing corporation. Then we will conclude with some bench marks and criteria for selection of profit-prone "converts" that may be comparable to *stocks that double in a year.*

Suppose, for example, you bought a $1,000 5-percent ten-year debenture of Wayout Instrument Company at par; and that the bond was convertible into the company's common stock at $50 a share any time until maturity. You had, unless the bond was called for redemption prior to maturity, the right either to continue holding that $1,000 bond or to convert it into 20 shares of Wayout common stock at any time. The bond provided you with a senior, and presumably safe, security, with a dependable interest return of $50 a year.

But you were not an investor — you were a speculator; and the only reason you bought Wayout convertible 5's was because you thought the stock would go up and that, in that event, you might convert (or sell) your bond at a handsome profit. At the time, however, Wayout common was selling at $40 a share and paying a $1 dividend. Obviously you would not convert because the 20 shares of Wayout common you could get by converting were worth (in total) only $800 in market value and the $20 annual income ($1 a share on 20 shares) was far below the $50 interest you were receiving. So conversion at the time was unprofitable.

Let's imagine, however, the passage of time, two or three years perhaps. Wayout Instrument in the meantime has prospered. The common stock now earns $4 a share, pays a $2 dividend, and sells on the market at $100 a share (25 times earnings). Now you're agog about the conversion potentials since 20 shares of Wayout common are worth $2,000. Your original $1,000 bond, by the magic of the conversion privilege, is selling at 210, or

$2,100, and you have a choice of selling (and doubling your money) or converting into the common stock. If you sell, you're out of the picture with a rewarding profit. If you convert, you'll give up forever your senior position as a bondholder and the $50 interest, and become instead a stockholding partner in Wayout, receiving $40 ($2 times 20 shares) in annual income. If the fortunes of Wayout are in a long-range uptrend, you may have a real winning stock — possibly a baby Occidental Petroleum, Xerox, or IBM. If you're a real dyed-in-the-wool speculator, however, you will probably sell your bond at 210, and look around for another attractive convert selling back around par that has a chance to emulate, duplicate, or even exceed the pleasing performance of Wayout.

From the above example, it's easy to see why converts are alluring to speculators. They have some interesting built-in advantages. As senior securities, they are less likely to decline drastically in bear markets than the common stocks they are tied to. The real "kicker," however, in convertible bonds is the fact that you can buy them largely on borrowed money and get a lot of leverage working for you. Until early 1967, it was possible to buy convertible bonds by putting down as little as 20 percent of their market value at a commercial bank. You could buy, as an illustration, ten $1,000 Wayout convertibles at par ($10,000) merely by putting up $2,000 of your own money. Then if the bond (impelled by its conversion value) went up to 120, you could sell the ten bonds for $12,000, pocket the $2,000 (a 100 percent profit on your $2,000) and get your $2,000 back. Your only costs would be brokerage plus about 6 percent interest on the $8,000 you borrowed, or $480 a year; against your coupon income from the bonds of $500.

Because, in the case of converts that go up, borrowing to buy them can be so profitable, this type of security has become enormously popular. There is a hitch, however, and that is that Federal Reserve credit regulations have changed in the past year and borrowing to buy securities from a bank on a 20 percent margin is no longer permitted. Many banks have discontinued making such new loans, or will make them only on much higher margins and at higher interest rates. A new Federal Reserve provision permits brokerage houses to make loans to clients on convertible bonds at the same terms as commercial banks (50 percent margin), so that even though margin requirements may be much higher for converts (they are 70 percent on stocks), it will still be possible to speculate by using a good chunk of somebody else's (your broker's) money to create leverage for you.

It is also to be observed that the downtrending stock market of early 1968 made this marginal speculation most hazardous. Some converts lost several points in a single day, and Control Data 5's (among the most volatile) fell 56 points in a single week! When the market is bearish, converts, especially those selling at high premiums (on a conversion, not an investment, basis), plunge along with stocks. "When they back up the wagon in a raid, everybody rides!"

To give you a sample shopping list of convertible bonds, we have selected the following issues at random from the market of April 26, 1968:

REPRESENTATIVE CONVERTIBLE BONDS

ISSUE	% RATE		SHARES PER $1,000 BOND	PRICE OF BOND	PRICE OF COMMON
Allied Super-markets	5 3/4	1987	51.95	107 3/4	16 3/4
Aluminum Co. of America	5 1/4	1991	11.76	108	72 3/4

Automatic Sprinkler	4 3/8	1987	16.95	83 5/8	38 1/8
Hart Schaffner & Marx	4 1/2	1992	23.53	124 1/2	53
Nytronics	6	1982	34.97	163	47 1/4
Radio Corp. of America	4 1/2	1992	16.95	107 1/2	52 1/8
	4 1/2	1992	16.95	107 1/2	52 1/8
Teledyne	3 1/2	1992	8.23	116	122 1/2
Unexcelled	5 3/4	1982	26.3	127	48 3/4

From the foregoing list, you might note that convertible bonds sell on a lower yield basis than "plain bonds" of the same quality. This is in anticipation of possible actual gains the conversion privilege may create. When the conversion has actual value, convertible bonds nearly always sell at a price above the aggregate value of the shares available on conversion. This higher price for the bond is again in anticipation of a higher price for the subject common. It also reflects the fact that speculators are generally willing to pay a premium for converts because they can (on borrowed money) control a greater number of common shares in the same company with fewer dollars than through an outright purchase of the subject stock on 70 percent margin.

CONVERTIBLE PREFERREDS

The same general principles apply to convertible preferred stocks as to convertible bonds. The preferred, however, although senior to common stock, is an equity, not a debt, security. In hard times, the dividend may be omitted on preferred shares, although most have cumulative provisions whereby if a dividend (or dividends) is missed in one year, it must be "made up" in a later one, and before the common stock receives a dividend. Thus, as a security for dependable income, the preferred is less highly prized than debentures, although in very large blue-chip companies, nobody worries about the continuity of preferred dividends. As an offset, however, preferred dividend rates have historically been higher than interest rates on bonds in the same company. (This has not been uniformly true in recent years because corporations and institutions enjoy certain exemptions from tax payment on dividends they receive from preferred stocks that do not apply in the case of bond interest.) On occasion, too, the convertible provisions built into preferred stocks are more attractive and rewarding than those of convertible bonds. Also, some preferreds are a little farther down the ladder in the financial structure of a corporation. These "second preferreds" receive their dividend payments only after the senior or first preferreds have been assured.

To illustrate representative convertible preferreds, we have selected at random the three below as of March 8, 1968:

ISSUE	DIVIDEND	CONVERTIBLE INTO	PREFERRED MARKET PRICE	PRICE OF COMMON
Diamond Shamrock No Par Convertible Preferred	$1.20	.45 share of common	11	44
Ideal Basic Industries $100 Par Cumulative	4.75	4.35 shares of common	16	78
Pet Incorporated No Par Cumulative Second Preferred	1.00	1/2 share of common	17 1/2	25

Of the above, the market action of Ideal might prove particularly impressive since each gain of one point in the common stock translates into a gain of 4.35 points on the preferred.

**CORPORATE FUNCTION OF
CONVERTIBLE SECURITIES**

The first major American corporation to offer a convertible bond was probably Southern Pacific Company early in the 1890's. Bonds of this type are issued in volume at two key stages of the business cycle: (1) in a depression or (2) toward or at the top of a bull market. In the first instance, convertible bonds are issued to creditors (usually holders of defaulted bonds) in bankruptcy or reorganization actions. Often the original face amount is scaled down, and the holder of a $1,000 defaulted bond will be offered $500 in a new income convertible bond. For example, St. Louis San Francisco in the Great Depression offered, in exchange for defaulted mortgage bonds, 4½ percent income bonds convertible into 30 shares of common. These worked out well and patient holders got back all the money they had lost in the old bonds, plus a sizable profit to boot, as St. Louis San Francisco common rose to happy heights many years later. Dozens of railway, industrial, and real estate convertible securities were spawned in the 1930's. Most of them have since been redeemed or converted, but it took years of patient waiting as forlorn companies struggled back from insolvency.

In good times, convertible bonds are issued by corporations because:

1. Converts are easier to sell and underwriting fees for distributing them are accordingly lower than for plain bonds.

2. Interest rates are lower. A convertible bond may pay 1 percent less interest than a nonconvertible debenture of the same investment grade.

3. The convert has a built-in capacity to "pay off" debt. When it is converted, debt and interest charges automatically disappear from the balance sheet.

4. The conversion rate is usually set at a price from 10 to 20 percent above the current quotation of the related stock at the time the bond is issued. Thus, in effect, the company issuing the bond is actually selling common stock (for future delivery) as much as 20 percent above the price it could get for it otherwise.

5. An issue of convertible bonds can be sold at a time when common-stock financing might be too uncertain or too costly. Many newer, younger companies with relatively unseasoned common stock can market sizable issues of bonds under market conditions wherein their stock could not be sold easily or in sufficient amounts to provide adequately for working capital and expansion needs.

6. Convertible bonds of strong companies can readily be sold to stockholders under a "rights" offering. American Telephone and Telegraph and many other large utilities have made regular use of convertible bonds at spaced intervals, as a part of long-range corporate financing programs.

THE BOOM IN CONVERTIBLE PREFERREDS

Until the past three years, preferred stocks were a dying commodity in the vineyards of corporation finance. About the only companies issuing them were utilities, which found this vehicle useful to raise a percentage of the needed new money, and to balance their corporate structures. Such utility preferred issues, however, were seldom made convertible.

Since 1965, however, with "conglomerates" surging on the scene and the "urge to merge" reaching epidemic proportions, the preferred stock has roared back into popularity, in convertible form, and there are now a hundred choice issues for you to choose from.

The convertible preferred is, in fact, almost built to order as the financial merchandise to be offered to shareholders of a "selling out" company. There are actually four practical ways for one company to buy another: (1) cash — so much a share for the subject common; (2) for notes or debentures; (3) for common stock, or (4) for convertible preferred.

Cash or debentures received by shareholders in the company being taken over create immediate taxable income in the form of a capital gain; and most stockholders prefer a tax-free exchange. The exchange of their shares for common in the buying company may not be acceptable if the common is unseasoned, has gyrated widely in the market, or pays a meager and insecure dividend. If investors sell out, they want to be sure the pieces of paper they get will not melt like butter in the noonday sun, and erode the paper profits produced by the exchange. In early 1968, a dozen major mergers foundered because the common stock of the aggressive conglomerate, offered as the exchange medium, fell off 25 percent or more and killed the deal. Occidental Petroleum and Signal Oil failed to merge because the market ratios between their shares were drastically and swiftly altered in a declining stock market.

Because under certain conditions common stock is neither attractive nor acceptable as "Chinese money" in a merger, many companies have authorized and offered new issues of convertible preferred to implement desired mergers. The preferred, being a senior security, provides better market defense on the down side than a common stock; the preferred dividend is often larger and usually more dependable than the dividend on the disappearing common stock, and the exchange of preferred for common stock is regarded by the Internal Revenue Service as a tax-free exchange, with no tax due or payable unless or until the preferred stock is sold. This may take place years later, or in selling the estate of the owner.

The three convertible preferred stocks listed earlier came into being via the merger route. Ideal Basic Preferred was offered for Potash Company of America common; Pet for Frank G. Shattuck Company; and Diamond for Shamrock Oil & Gas Corporation.

CRITERIA

Convertible securities are a proper part of the arsenal of weapons for the eager speculator striving to double his money in a year. Not just any convert will do, however. If you expect to glean generous profits, keep these criteria in mind in screening your selections in the convertible category:

1. Buy the convert (bond or preferred) at a price as close as possible to what it would sell for if it had no conversion feature. You are most likely to do this when the issue first hits the market.

2. Make sure the company is a money-maker and rapidly increasing its earnings. If the convert you're looking at relates to a dull common stock, with no reasonable hope for gain in earnings in the next eighteen months, you'd better shift your gaze elsewhere.

3. Buy in dynamic companies for dynamic gains; but get some strong assurance that the whole market is in an ascendant phase or you'll be stuck with your convert, no matter how good it is theoretically.

4. Pick companies with relatively small amounts of common outstanding. Issues with a "small float" will go up faster on good news and develop scarcity value if company progress is outstanding.

5. When you've made your score, sell the convert and look around for another at a much lower price to replace it.

6. Be nimble and don't hem and haw in making up your mind to sell when you have made a satisfactory profit. You've lost the traditional downside protection of a senior security when it's selling at 200!

7. Borrow on your converts (bonds are far better for borrowing) to increase leverage; but don't go so deeply in hock that a market downspin can ruin you. And don't answer a margin call. Sell instead! Good luck, and may you pick nothing but doublers—unless it's a tripler or quadrupler.

10
bull markets and bare knees

Off and on during the past forty years, there have appeared in the financial press or in market letters of brokerage houses recurrent conjectures or whimsical observations that there exists a definite relationship between the height of the hemline of women's dresses in any given year and the levels of stock prices.

SKIRTS AND NATIONAL INCOME
Since 1958, the H. W. Gossard Company, a renowned maker of ladies' corsets and lingerie, has published annually a chart featuring the trendline of national income since 1900, accompanied by sketches of young ladies dressed in the prevailing fashions of each era. These sketches appear above the high and low points on the chart when national income reached a new historic peak

and when it fell back to a cyclical bottom in transition years. The Gossard theory also asserts that tight waists accompany lower hemlines.

This chart, available from Gossard, has attracted considerable attention. It tends to validate the general theory that hemlines rise in good times and fall in recessions. This study, however newsworthy and provocative of comment, makes no precise correlations, since it does not portray models and hemlines for successive calendar years. Moreover, it is geared to the national income statistical series, not nearly as sensitive or widely followed as the Dow-Jones Industrial Stock Average covering the same years.

On December 15, 1964, Mr. Vermont Royster, editor of *The Wall Street Journal,* published a merry column entitled "Boom or Bust," which reflected on the possible relationship between hemlines and buoyant markets. He concluded: "Hemlines vary directly with the rise and fall of GNP."

In May, 1967, Harris Upham & Company, a leading nationwide brokerage firm, presented in its market letter a chart showing the yearly Dow-Jones Industrial Average from 1897 to date, with sketches of young women, in the mode of the year, above or below key high or low points on the stock trendline. These pictures document fairly well, visually, the idea that skirts rise in a manner somewhat parallel to stocks in bull markets; and plunge downward when stocks do. For example, in 1929, stocks and dresses were both high; in 1932, they were both just off the floor.

This was all jolly good fun, and the Harris Upham Hemline Indicator inspired many comments in the daily and weekly financial press.

In fact, somewhat earlier (July, 1965), the Economics Department of McGraw-Hill, Inc., publishers of *Business Week,* had issued a three-page report, without charts, highlighting high hemlines as a recurrent phenomenon of prosperous times — and vice versa — but without any specific reference to stocks.

UP AND DOWN TOGETHER

And there the matter has stood until I could endure the uncertainty no longer. I simply had to find out if there was any sense at all to this hemline theory. Have skirts indeed gone up historically when stocks did? Did they go relatively higher or lower than stocks? And, most particularly, which came first, the rise in hemlines or in stocks? In other words, will the real market barometer please stand up?

To answer properly these nagging questions, I obviously had to have something more substantial than pictures to rely on. The Dow-Jones Industrial Average chart could of course be plotted accurately from actual sales prices of stocks, day after day and year after year. But how could I present a hemline curve that could be drawn on the same chart and in some sort of comparative relationship with DJIA? If the theory was valid, obviously the two lines should look much alike.

Accordingly I did some research. I designed a novel chart expressing annual hemline variations in inches off the floor.

With appropriate humility, I present in this chapter, in chart form, the answer to the question: "Skirts and Stocks — Up and Down Together?" While I certainly do not claim to have originated this theory (I don't think anyone knows who did), I am the first to chart its linear proof — to convert conjecture into credibility!

THE NATURAL AFFINITY BETWEEN FASHION AND FINANCE

Before this earth-shaking, or at least hip-shaking, chart is unveiled, however, it may be well to see how dresses and stocks ever became linked in the first place. The relationship derives from a long-term affinity between fashion and money.

When somebody mentions the word "fashion," it seems invariably to refer to the current popular style in women's apparel. Actually, however, fashion — the new mode, the "in" thing — is all about us. In addition to miniskirts and bikinis, and pipestem trousers for men, current fashion embraces equally our whole way of life — cookouts', op and pop art, hippies, color TV, shaggy-haired young men, performance stocks, tall socks, rock-and-roll, condominiums, scuba diving, surfing, credit cards, and Everett Dirksen!

To be more precise, fashion is a concomitant of money possession, which makes possible leisure time, a thirst for culture, and a social compulsion to keep up with or, better yet, to top someone. Cadillacs beat Chevies, chinchilla beats mink, a brownstone beats a penthouse, and the Mets beat nobody!

Women's fashions are actually a comparatively modern phenomenon, and for our purposes they did not become significant until after World War I. We are principally interested in the past fifty years of fashion, 1917-1966. Why this period? Because before that ladies' fashions were a minor influence in our economy, and the only women who really spent any time and money at it were women of royalty or the theater; or women socially important because of their relationship to men of position, power, or opulence, often as mistresses as well as wives.

Further, it should be observed that high fashion did not involve the excitement of radically changing hemlines until well into the twentieth century. Almost all stylish skirts until 1914 had hemlines dragging along the floor or perhaps two or three inches above. Equally, until after 1915, stock prices were, with few exceptions, attracting very little popular attention or following. Holders of common stocks were probably only a little more numerous than ladies who could afford, and sported, high fashion.

NEW YORK CITY: FASHION AND FINANCE CENTER

It is in part for these reasons that the chart midstream in this chapter, around which the whole theory is developed, begins in 1917 and not before. At or about that year, two economic institutions had become solidly established. They document and refine our theory about the affinity between fashion and finance. These twin phenomena were the confirmed position of New York as (1) the financial center of America and (2) the ladies' fashion center of America. The rising statures of both as (1) big business and (2) daily topics of conversation and discussion in American homes increased as wealth became diffused, and per-capita incomes steadily rose.

Higher incomes have indeed placed new millions of women each decade in a position to be patrons of fashion and of Wall Street; and the garment industry accommodated them by designing fashionable ready-made dresses, manufactured in volume, and within the budget of middle- and lower-middle-class families. The arrival and concentration in New York City of thousands of emigrants from Central and Eastern Europe, many of them tailors by trade, built in due course a vast garment industry on "Seventh Avenue," an industry that today sells annually well over $5 billion wholesale in women's dresses, suits, coats, sportswear, and blouses—not including uniforms, undergarments, and children's wear.

On the financial side, there were in 1917 only 613 stocks listed on the New York Stock Exchange, with total value below $30 billion. Today there are 1,700 issues listed, worth, at the 1967 year end, $605.8 billion. In 1917, there were approximately 500,000 stockholders in America. Today there are 24 million (more than 50 percent women), plus 4½ million holders of mutual funds, and probably 100 million others who own stocks indirectly through their interests in insurance policies, pension, welfare or retirement funds.

LIMITS

We have gathered the above data to establish a background relationship between fashion and finance, skirts and stocks. We admit, however, to having narrowed the fields a little to suit our purposes. Obviously fashion is something more than skirts. It's also fabrics, silhouettes, sportswear, furs, handbags, shoes, gloves, and hats. But we can't measure all these phenomena against stock prices. If, for instance, we used bikinis as a gauge, we'd have the Dow-Jones Industrial Average at 3,000 right now; and at 3,500 for topless models!

Equally, finance is more than stocks. It's bank loans and deposits, mortgages, bonds, leaseholds, royalties, trust funds, etc. But again, stock prices are clearly measurable and volatile and newsworthy; and they do display vertical action, long thought to be similar in time and relative extent to the varying altitudes of skirts.

On the style side, it's just too bad we couldn't work into the chart such eye-catching fashion phenomena as waistlines and necklines, but frankly, there appears to be no coherent or measurable trend in these. There is a little evidence, however, that plunging necklines and plunging stock markets occur in the same general time period — sort of a peek and valley theory!

Levity aside, we're now about to introduce our long-awaited chart, with just one additional explanation. In plotting hemline heights, we got the altitude figures from models of daytime dresses in style in each of the fifty years; and the distances off the ground relate to a woman of average height, about 5'7" — approximately the size twelve misses' dress that is standard in the trade.

Now, here for the first time is a chart designed to answer the question of the hour:

Skirts and Stocks —

Up and Down Together?

Yes!

bull markets . . .

Introducing THE HEMLINE INDEX
OF STOCK PRICES

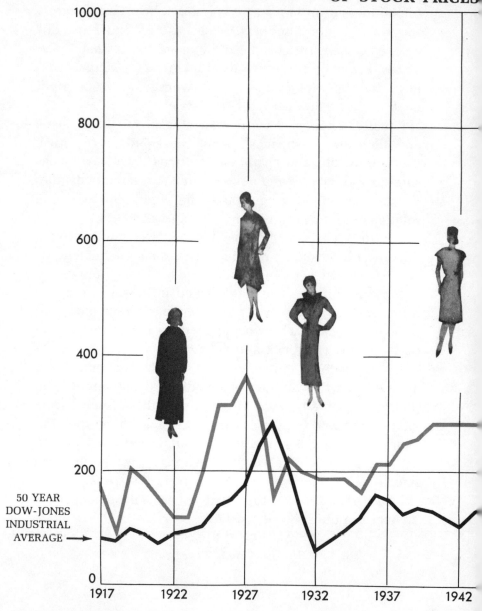

50 YEAR
DOW-JONES
INDUSTRIAL
AVERAGE →

and bare knees!

HEMLINE
IN
INCHES
OFF
THE
← FLOOR

30

20

10

0

1947 1952 1957 1962 1967

COMMENT ON THE CHART

By starting with the year 1917, we can present a fifty-year comparison; and that year marks approximately the beginning of broad national share markets, and of consumer spending on fashions in such volume as to affect and reflect national growth and prosperity. That year was, moreover, the start of war prosperity, with rising wages and a broadening investor class getting its introduction to marketable securities through purchase of Liberty Bonds.

Business had actually begun to improve and stocks begun a rising trend in 1915. This upswing appears to have been foretold by shorter skirts, so that in 1915 there appeared for the first time in this century hemlines 8 inches off the floor. They continued to rise, along with stocks, until 1919.

Then hemlines started down somewhat ahead of stocks in anticipation of the 1920-21 depression; after which both stocks and hems reversed. Between 1925 and 1926, skirts reached knee length, the highest altitude up to that time.

If we seek to apply hemlines as a prophetic barometer for stock prices, 1927 is a good year to analyze. There were, in that year of prosperity, speakeasies, a new car named the Chrysler, flappers, and a definite trend to longer dresses. This downtrend in hemlines was, in effect, a strong signal of declining stock prices to come, and preceded, by about two and a half years, the topping out of the stock market in October, 1929. Had the hemline chart been available then, perhaps it would have prevented, for tens of thousands, the financial baths they were otherwise doomed to take between 1929 and 1932.

TURNING POINTS

There was a gradual but definite uptrend in skirt lines beginning in late 1932 and extending, with a pause for the slowdown in 1936-37, to 8 inches off the ground again in 1939, and reaching the ogling level of 15 inches in 1940. Here again was another powerful directional signal, although this time not given so far in advance as in 1927.

The war period put style on the sidelines. Millions of women became war workers, and their styles of dress were consequently heavily functional. Shorter skirts were dictated by two necessities. First there was the need for greater mobility in feminine action — riding buses to work, operating at workbenches and assembly lines, where flowing dresses and fancy sleeves would have been inconvenient or hazardous. The second factor limiting the free play of fashion trends during the war was a government restriction on production of civilian fabrics, which limited garments to 3½ yards of cloth, and skirt widths to 64 inches; and fashion stood still for almost five years. The plain lines of the shirtwaist dress became the mode, and slacks and overalls were almost a uniform for women factory workers.

After World War II, the pent-up desires of women to look more feminine and to spend a larger percentage of individual and family incomes on clothes led to an eager resurgence of fashion consciousness. Return to a civilian economy took a little time; the stock market was in a tentative and generally negative trend. Correspondingly, hemlines declined from wartime levels — a trend authenticated in 1947 with the introduction of the "New Look," featuring curvaceous silhouettes, longer and more flowing skirts, and pinched-in waists. These lower skirt lines foretold the lower stock market of 1949 with considerable advance notice.

The 1950's witnessed a general rise in the Dow-Jones Industrial Average, checked in 1953, and again in 1956. The hemlines rather accurately reflected this uptrend, with the long dresses of 1950-51 giving place to rising hemlines, especially noticeable in 1954 (indicating the end of the short recession of 1953); and continuing higher until 1958, when hemlines descended moderately, as did stocks, for a couple of years. In October, 1961, skirts were close to knee high again, which seemed to say that the dip in stock prices occurring ten months later was by no means the end of the long-term bull market. Thus skirts continued to rise, topping off with the miniskirt, which first appeared at about the time the DJIA reached an all-time closing high of 995.15 on February 9, 1966. Hemlines continued to rise and so did the market in the period between October, 1966, and summer, 1967 — which brings our chart comparison almost to the present.

Reviewing the charts, we can now state with considerable assurance that there does exist a demonstrable relationship between skirts and stocks and, in general, hemlines are the "lead" barometer.

FUTURE ALTITUDES AND ATTITUDES

The future of the skirt-line chart and its validity and acceptance as a respected market barometer are clouded by the near-ceiling represented by mid-1967 hemlines. The prevailing fanny-high minidress leaves little room for the hemline to rise on the chart, to correspond with, say, a 1,500 figure on the DJIA. By historic hem-price relationships, stock prices "have gone about as far as they can go." The next indicated phase should be downward, because (1) skirt lines cannot decently go higher and (2) indicated styles promulgated by certain fashion designers for fall, 1967, call for longer dresses. Indeed, we may have established a new Wall Street slogan to guide market decisions of avid traders: "Don't sell till you see the heights of their thighs!"

A decline in hemlines preceding, or accompanied by, a decline in stock prices can of course be accommodated within the limits of the present chart. We do, however, face a problem for the future. Granted that we have, over a fifty-year period, established a plausible relationship between stocks and skirts, how can we portray this relationship graphically if or when the DJIA advances to 1,500 or higher? While there is no theoretical ceiling on stock prices, there is an obvious ceiling on dress heights. Skirts and stocks may well continue to go up and down in some sort of parallel relationship in the years ahead, so we have developed an adjusted formula to correlate hemlines to DJIA if that average rises above 1,100.

This revised formula would not destroy the validity of our theory, but would simply reflect hemlines on a more sensitive scale — and keep them from zooming upward off the chart! The comparative result would be quite like the use of logarithmic paper for plotting bar charts.

PSYCHOLOGICAL BACKGROUND

So far, we have treated these two exciting phenomena, skirts and stock variations, as cold statistical data like spring-wheat or pig-iron prices, tied together only by the fact that both are money oriented. The extensive purchase of fashionwear and stock occurs only in opulent societies. (Incidentally, in 1966, American women spent $7 billion on clothes; men, less than half that!)

On reflection, and with a modicum of research, we can conclude that there are powerful psychological forces making skirts and stocks go up and down together. Market swings and fashion changes are both motivated quite as much by emotional factors as by money logic. Both may well be expected to reflect happiness, confidence, and hope, as well as fear, anxiety, and gloom. Hence, in good times we see confidence reflected in a nationwide amorous zeal, or at least more animated girl watching. We know this to be true because, in civilized countries, birth rates rise during prosperity and fall during depressions. This romantic zest is no doubt stimulated by possession or acquisition of more money (rising income and speculative profits), making possible more extravagant expenditures on feminine plumage, and fashions tending toward higher skirts to sustain and encourage wolfish ogling. Perhaps, too, the fashion turn to lower skirts is a necessity in economic declines, tending to make men pay more attention to business.

Another observable phenomenon is that higher skirts, symbolizing euphoria, confidence, and hope, are linked emotionally to brighter, livelier colors. If you doubt this, think of the miniskirts of 1967. Were there ever assembled on the female form such dazzling arrays of gaudy colors — pastels, pinks, yellows, reds, purples? As a by-product, business prosperity is promoted by higher stocks, and a greater assortment of designs and fabric, not to mention underthings, which must be bought because of their occasional visibility and their corresponding need to match, or blend with, outerthings. The short-dress fashion economy is also stimulated by the need for larger handbags, to serve as "modesty panels" discreetly deployed across the knees of ladies, particularly when riding buses!

If psychological spurs can be found to account for rising trends in skirts and stocks, they can influence attitudes just as well in reverse — in recessions or depressions. As skirts go down, quite possibly romantic enthusiasms cool down accordingly. And the longer skirts are invariably made of heavier fabrics, and in darker, less lively colors — browns, blacks, dark grays. In 1932, as the chart shows, stocks were very low, skirts were very low, and the fashionable colors of the year were somber — some almost funereal.

PROJECTION

Ultimately the pendulum will swing. It always has. Women tire of the same style, colors and fabrics, and in due course they will demand a change, if only out of caprice or boredom. Men, too, welcome a change in their women. This psychological or emotional urge to change (from fashions in stocks as well as fashions in clothes) may in fact be the key to our entire theory. If indeed women's styles do change their trendlines ahead of stocks, then we should be most vigilant in observing whether the current fashionable dress designs, or those projected for the next spring or fall, are going up or down. Whichever way they are headed may well indicate the direction of stock prices in the months ahead — and influence market decisions.

In the first quarter of 1968, we had a kind of schizophrenia in skirts. The young, the jet, and the hippie set wore miniskirts of maximum brevity, 28 inches off the floor. At the same time, matrons and younger matrons displayed at many exclusive social events hemlines lowered to the knee or midcalf, which hinders calculation of the 1968 formula. Dress styles may now have become dual, and an average between them may in the future be needed to correlate with stock prices. In any event, it would be our opinion in summer, 1968, that miniskirts are still the dominant factor and that accordingly there will be a rising and roaring bull market in 1969, carrying Dow-Jones to 1,200. Hemlines precede, in their motion and direction, the rise or fall of stocks.

11

the corporate hunter and his quarry

The year 1967 will be remembered, among other things, as the year of the takeover. Over 2,900 significant corporate acquisitions were recorded, and 1968-69 appears certain to carry on this fashion for financial marriages. The only visible slowdown was occasioned by a languid stock market, dimming the luster of some noted mergers in the first quarter of 1968.

We discussed, in the chapter on conglomerates, some of the reasons for the current spate of mergers: the urge to build companies of greater resources and stature; increasing rates of corporate growth; application of gifted management over wider areas of operation; creation of stronger credit, more efficient buying, cost and account controls; and, finally, the attraction of more stockholders, stimulating market trading in the conglomerate's common in great volume and at exalted price/earnings multiples.

Takeovers have, indeed, become a new way of business life that may eventually change the whole economic scene by displacing a boatload of older executives and raising legal and regulatory questions, not only along antitrust lines but with regard to corporate financial policy in the nation. When a large and voracious enterprise seeks control or ownership of another and usually smaller one, what are the steps to be taken? Who will protect the interests of minority shareholders? What will prevent outright manipulation in the shares of the quarry company if a group buys up the floating supply of shares and heralds a big "possible merger" in the financial press, and then cancels the merger proposal, while informed insiders sell out their earlier acquired shares at a tidy profit? After that, the shares of the quarry company may dive dismally.

A great deal more will be heard on these questions in the months ahead. Meanwhile, speculators should be constantly on the lookout for companies which may be takeover bait, and may create swift market gains for the perceptive and the nimble who acquire stock early and sell shrewdly. The opportunity to double your money in takeover stocks occurs in dozens of instances in each bull-market year. In 1967, for example, General Development Corporation, in which City Investing acquired over a 40 percent interest, rose from a low of 6 to a high of 18⅞; Sheraton Corporation, sought and bought by International Telephone, went from 8¾ to 32⅛; Symington Wayne, a rather mundane company, rose from 20⅛ to 45, after a tender offer by Dresser Industries to buy Symington at $40 a share. Allis-Chalmers moved between 20⅜ and 41; and turned down a tender of $45 from Ling-Temco-Vought.

HOW TO SELECT QUARRY COMPANIES

Obviously, in your quest to make money on shares in companies to be bought out, you cannot pick at random among actively traded issues. You have to develop some criteria for screening and selection. What are these criteria? How can you tell in advance that a particular company may be aggressively sought (and at much higher prices) by one or more companies on the prowl?

Here are some of the general characteristics of merger-bait companies:

1. A high and solid book value, preferably rich in cash or marketable securities.

2. A low current price/earnings multiple.

3. A tired, incompetent, or lazy management, or a company shot through with dissension so that the presumably talented management team of the buying company could replace "old fogies" and expand profits thereby.

4. A flat or declining earnings trend within the preceding two years, which causes the company's shares to be quoted at rather bargain prices.

5. A company having products, services, markets coverage, or research capabilities that complement the production and merchandising pattern of the proposed parent.

6. A management that owns relatively few shares. This permits a stock to be bought readily from many stockholders, none of whom owns enough stock to protest effectively or to block the merger. (Allis-Chalmers was hot bait because its entire management owned less than 10,000 shares.)

7. A company with valuable and strategically located land, oil, or mineral holdings; or one owning important licenses, patents, formulas, or marketing contracts.

8. A company with unusually gifted management. (Some mergers are engineered almost solely to acquire administrative, sales, scientific, or technological talents.)

9. A company that can earn and grow faster as part of a big organization (possibly benefiting from the production facilities, sales organization, research, or resources) than by staying by itself.

10. A company with a tax-loss carry-forward that can benefit the net-profit picture of the acquiring company in a very special way.

11. A company run by one or a small group of older men who are ready, willing, or eager to retire and to realize sizable capital gains by exchange of their shares for cash, common or convertible preferred stock in the seeking company.

While the above list is not complete, it does outline most of the reasons why companies sell out, and why merger-minded companies search for them.

The steps in acquisitions commonly observed are as follows: (1) A steady and usually well concealed buying of the subject shares in the market before anything is said publicly. (2) A cash-tender offer of a certain figure for a specified number of shares, or a share-exchange offer. The tender offer is almost invariably 15 to 25 percent above the trading range of the stock at the time the offer is made. (3) Since by this time the intentions of the seeker have become well known, either the potential buyer and seller-out sit down together and negotiate details of a deal or majority-share purchase, or the management of the quarry company may bleat loudly against the predations of the presumed financial octopus. (4) In the meantime, some other hungry conglomerate may muddy the waters by throwing in another, higher, bid, which makes a lot of headlines on the financial pages. (5) Finally, a merger or takeover is concluded (most frequently, nowadays, by an offer of convertible preferred), or thwarted, or deferred; or dead due to changes in market conditions, or the minds of managements; then the quarry company resumes its status quo ante or remains "up for grabs."

GEORGE J. MEYER MANUFACTURING COMPANY

To illustrate some of the points we have been making, we propose to examine a specific case. George J. Meyer Manufacturing Company is an excellent old-line Milwaukee-based company, a worldwide and diversified manufacturer of automatic packaging equipment, and the nation's number-one producer of automatic machinery for filling bottles and cans for the domestic soft-drink and beer industries.

Under the five-year presidency (1963-67) of George L. N. Meyer, Jr., grandson of the founder, the company had made excellent progress both internally and by acquisitions (a palletizing company and an automatic sortation company were acquired in 1964; and a 51 percent interest in Logan Company, Louisville, Kentucky, a leading maker of high-quality high-efficiency conveyor systems was acquired in 1966). In the five years, sales had expanded by $30 million, to $63,389,000 for the fiscal year ending 6/30/67. At that date, book value of Meyer common stood at $33.57 per share and net earnings for fiscal 1967 were $2.80 a share. The stock in mid-September was selling at around $32 a share (just about book value) and about 12 times its net earnings.

The thirty-eight-year-old Mr. Meyer had ambitions for the company and sought to be ready to negotiate compatible acquisitions. To this end he proposed that at the annual meeting of shareholders of the company on October 30, 1967, they should consider and approve the authorization of 300,000 shares of a new no par preferred stock. This was designed to provide an attractive financial vehicle to offer in future acquisitions and required an amendment to the articles of incorporation and an affirmative vote of 66⅔ percent of common stocks. At the meeting, approval of this new preferred was not given. Within the next thirty days, Meyer dipped as low as 27 bid on the over-the-counter market. The financial community apparently viewed bearishly the failure to create this new preferred stock, regarded as a vital tool in the company's merger program.

The attractive "numbers" outlined above, and the fact that the stock had fallen several points below its book value to a market price only 10 times earnings, became a signal for corporate pouncing. First, in November, 1967, Bath Industries, a Maine shipbuilder and manufacturer of heavy machinery, announced a plan to acquire 70 percent of Meyer by a tender offer of $42 a share. This was given wide press notice and evoked from Meyer management a statement typical of such cases: "Directors have taken the position that we are not for sale." The Bath offer, however, stimulated OTC market interest in Meyer common and the stock advanced swiftly from a low bid of 27 to the high 30's. Before the Bath offer was given official consideration in depth by either Meyer management or stockholders, another contender came on the scene—Automatic Sprinkler Corporation. This aggressive conglomerate topped the Bath offer for 70 percent of Meyer common, by proposing to give one share of Automatic Sprinkler common for each of the 719,750 shares of George J. Meyer outstanding. This offer was announced on November 29. The preceding day, the closing price of Automatic Sprinkler common on the New York Stock Exchange was $54, indicating a total offer of about $38.8 million for the Meyer company; and giving Meyer common a theoretical value of $54.

Through acquisitions, Automatic Sprinkler, a manufacturer of fire and industrial protection systems, hydraulic equipment, electronic instrumentation, and power systems, had grown rapidly. For the first nine months of 1967, it had reported sales of $125,248,000 against $52,500,000 for the same nine-month period in 1966. Harry J. Figgie, Jr., president of Automatic Sprinkler, had come to be regarded as one of the more gifted shepherds of conglomerates and, quite naturally, the Automatic Sprinkler offer had much allure for Meyer shareholders. On the strength of it they had already seen their stock move from 39 to around 50, OTC. Many Meyer holders felt that ATO (Automatic's New York Stock Exchange symbol) offered a better opportunity for further market advance than did their own common.

During January, 1968, Automatic Sprinkler common advanced to a high of $74 a share and Meyer common traded, OTC, as high as 71. It more than doubled in price between October, 1967, and February, 1968, proving what we mentioned earlier: quarry-company stocks, shrewdly traded, can fulfill our definition of *happiness*.

These heady market prices for ATO common were based in part on advanced estimates of its per share earnings for 1967 as between $1.80 and $2.00. On Wednesday, February 14, 1968, however, Automatic Sprinkler reported preliminary 1967 earnings of only $1.43 per share on an average of 5.2 million common shares outstanding. This figure failed to equal the more than 40 percent gain in the year's earnings predicted earlier in the year by Mr. Figgie, and Automatic Sprinkler sold off to 40⅜ on Friday, February 16.

Meanwhile, a prospectus outlining the exchange offer had been mailed to Meyer shareholders on February 13, calling for a vote on the merger at a stockholders' meeting to be held March 4. The original offer of exchange, share for share, of Meyer for Automatic Sprinkler contained, however, a provision that if ATO common sold at an average price of less than $50 a share in the fifteen days immediately before the effective date of the merger, additional ATO shares would be issued to Meyer stock owners to equal an average closing market value of $50 over that fifteen-day period.

This turned out to be expensive for ATO and protective for Meyer holders, because ATO common in March skidded below $30 a share. The meeting to approve the merger was delayed and, finally, on March 29, Meyer shareholders approved, and under the formula each Meyer share was to be exchanged for 1.6 shares of ATO; and Meyer common sold in the OTC market at $43 a share, reflecting this conclusion.

Here we have recounted an entire acquisition story, documenting solidly the opportunities that await you if you select, and make early investment in, a company that has merger appeal. As this was written, there are plenty of companies still around that may lose their identities in 1968-69, even perhaps before this book goes to press. Possible candidates would include St. Regis Paper (maybe some big oil company would like this), Racine Hydraulics, Guardian Chemical, Westinghouse Air Brake, National Chemsearch, fifty life-insurance companies, thirty computer-service companies, twenty realty companies, a couple of dozen small electronic companies, ten modest-sized oil-producing companies, and some hospital, medical supply, and scientific companies. So keep your eyes open for unnoticed companies with the specifications cited in the opening pages of this chapter.

12

growth stocks for possible doubling

In the past decade, growth stocks have fascinated Wall Street, and investors were well on their way to rich market rewards if they owned and held such dazzling performers as IBM, Xerox, Syntex, Cenco Instruments, McGraw-Hill, Occidental Petroleum, Litton, Solitron, Teledyne, etc. Such authentic growth issues have not only rewarded patient long-term holders well, but also turned in outstanding performances within a single year. For example, Fairchild Camera in 1965 rose from 27½ to 150½, a gain of 447.3 percent!

Futher, an examination of the annual performance of outstanding stocks in the past six years reveals that an important percentage of them were growth stocks. Accordingly, in our search for stocks that can double within a year, it's important to be able to pick out growth stocks from their less animate brethren.

CHARACTERISTICS OF GROWTH STOCKS

As a general rule, growth stocks are found in growing industries. In 1967, the "hot" industries were computers and scientific companies, and the outstanding performers were in these two stellar groups. Growth industries today would be electronics, real estate, space-age companies, computers, publishing, hospital supply, convalescent homes, apparel, beverages, prepared foods, water treatment, service companies, motels, leisure time, oil drillers, metals, oceanography. These industries are all growing far faster than the Gross National Product. They fill rising demands generated by the population explosion and the constant and substantial uptrend in per-capita incomes throughout the free world.

It does not follow, however, that all common stocks of companies located in growth industries are automatically growth stocks. Far from it. There are stragglers, marginal members, duds, and nonsurvivors even in the most rapidly expanding economic sectors. Over eight hundred motorcar companies have been formed since 1900. These all were in one of the most amazing growth industries the world has ever known. Yet how many of their stocks proved to be rewarding growth stocks? There are only four significant American motorcar companies today. As a growth stock, General Motors has been a dazzler; but whatever became of Moon, Marmon, Jackson, Velie, Dort, Dobie, and Franklin? A growth company must document, first, its capacity to survive and, second, its ability to earn and expand profits at an inordinate rate.

Equally, not all growth stocks are found in growing industries. In the coal industry, for instance, there has been a long-range decline since 1925, yet some splendidly growing companies and historic market performers have emerged in this fading economic sector — Peabody Coal and Joy Manufacturing (coal machinery), for example.

BENCH MARKS

One good way to select growth stocks is to seek the best-managed and most profitable companies in zooming industries. These may not be the largest units in their group, and, for our purposes, smaller companies in an early corporate phase are often the most dramatic gainers. It is, for example, much easier for a company to double its sales from $10 million annually to $20 million than for a larger company to go from $100 million to $200 million in sales. Small and middle-sized companies usually grow fastest. These are more difficult to pick out since they are less well known, appear on few investment or brokerage house recommended lists, and their shares often trade inactively in the over-the-counter market. Growth is always most dynamic in its earlier phases. A child grows much faster between one and ten than between ten and twenty!

With the above background guidelines in mind, we are now ready to list the particular qualities or characteristics we should seek in growth stocks that may lead to swift market gains within a single year.

CRITERIA FOR SELECTION OF GROWTH STOCKS

1. A growth stock should show a sales expansion at the rate of at least 12 percent annually compounded.

2. Net earnings should be increasing at a rate of at least 12 percent a year compounded; and net profits should rise at a faster rate than sales.

3. The favored industry should be growing at least twice as fast as the economy as a whole.

4. Growth should be not only rapid but consistent. An erratic company that increases its net earnings 70 percent one year and 5 percent the next would not qualify. Investors and market traders are partial to growth stocks like IBM, where substantial gains in net have been recorded *without interruption* year after year.

5. Management should be aggressive, intelligent, research minded, cost conscious, and energetic. In early-phase companies, driving management is often supplied by ambitious younger men trained and successful in big companies who seek larger rewards and greater personal freedom as part owners and directors of their own companies. Good management, as we have said, is often the lengthened shadow of a single outstanding individual: "Tex" Thornton at Litton Industries, the late Thomas Watson at IBM, Alfred Sloan at General Motors, Dr. Emery Lang at Polaroid, Robert Hensley at Life of Kentucky, Dr. Armand Hammer at Occidental Petroleum, Leon Hess at Hess Oil, for example. Betting on a business genius can be one of the most rewarding techniques for long-range or shorter-term market success.

6. The management group should be made up of large stockholders. If a substantial amount of stock (usually 30 percent or more) is held by management men, then they are likely to work hard to build wealth through capital gains on their stock. A hungry, stock-minded management is a common characteristic of a growth company.

7. Plowback is very important. Growth companies go in heavily for retained earnings, and the fastest-growing ones seldom pay out more than 40 percent of their net in cash in any year. Of all the companies whose stocks have doubled in a single year, very few will be found that pay out over 40 percent of net in cash.

This conservation of cash and reinvestment of profits

is, in fact, epidemic among growth companies. Retention of funds makes it less necessary to seek new outside capital for expansion, often diluting stockholders' equity, and it is also favored by high-bracket stockholders, who prefer market gains, taxable at only 25 percent, to cash dividends, taxable at 50 percent or higher. Heavy annual plowback builds up book value and expands future earning power; it also promotes higher market quotations of the subject common stocks.

8. In a well-managed growth company, profit margins (conversion of gross into net) are consistently high; and there is usually a tendency for profit margins to widen. In fact, even though sales are rising, if profit margins have declined noticeably for two or more years in a row, you're probably in the wrong growth stock!

9. A good growth company should show a consistently high return on stockholders' equity (the book value of its common stock). As a general rule, a growth company should earn not less than 15 percent on stockholders' equity annually. This percentage might dip in a single year due to unusual corporate expenditure for new facilities, or to costly research of a new product; but as a rule, performance stocks will earn 15 to 25 percent on stock equity with considerable regularity.

10. Growth stocks, to generate market gains, must be bought prudently, and preferably in early corporate phases. It's perfectly possible to pay too much even for the best growth stock. A friend of mine lost $80,000 in 1962 buying IBM at 555 and seeing it melt miserably in the erosive June market sun of that year. Growth stocks should be bought, if possible, before they have become widely acclaimed in the market, and preferably at a price/earnings multiple of no more than 15. Market prices of 60 and 70 times earnings are frequently overvaluations, discounting the growth factor too far into the future. Most growth-stock buyers, whether they purchase for a

trading swing (our approach) or for a long-term gain, develop some notions about future market potentials. The desired market action is for a growth stock, because it has become fashionable, to increase its price/earnings multiple steeply.

THE PLUS FACTOR

Obviously, in the stocks we seek, some special stimulation must take place. We should always be looking for some plus factor that may make the issue perform not just well but sensationally. The particular stock we look for should resemble Kentucky Fried Chicken, which, on remarkable earnings, rose from an original subscription price of $15 (in April, 1966) to well past $30 in less than six months, and to over $150 in two years. Occidental Petroleum, Poloron, University Computing, Data Processing Financial and General, Sheraton, Hilton, and EG&G all doubled in 1967 because their earnings surged and their multiples rose. This is not an official list of growth-type companies (we have a screened list of forty diversified selections for possible 100 percent gain later on in the book). The growth companies cited simulate the dynamics of growth that, in the past, have generated unusual stock profits.

In all this discussion about growth stocks, however, it must be observed that there is nothing eternal about growth. A company can expand remarkably for a few years and then either stop growing or go into a tailspin. The bowling industry, and its leaders, such as Brunswick and American Machine & Foundry, illustrate this. In 1959-60, it appeared that America was going to do nothing in its spare time but bowl, and these two companies surged ahead in the market, turning out bowling equipment and helping to finance hundreds of new bowling emporia, complete with automatic pin-spotters, restaurant facilities, and the rest of the works. When the bowling mania subsided, stocks in what had seemed a dazzling growth industry cooled off, and American Machine and Brunswick stockholders saw market profits in these issues vanish like snow upon the desert's dusty wastes.

The roster of growth stocks changes from year to year. In 1965, it was air transport and TV companies; in 1966, few companies could buck the downtrend. In 1967, computers, land and realty companies, scientific companies, conglomerates, and merger baits headed the list.

What about 1968-69? Our guess would be that growth-stock darlings will be found in oceanography, medical supply and hospital care, land companies, the life-insurance and mutual-fund combinations, measurement and instrumentation companies, certain oils, and metals— nickel, silver, and gold particularly—but not railroads! Do a little homework on some of these industries, and locate the standout companies in them, and you may find potential doublers.

13

doublers on the new york and american stock exchanges 1962-64

This chapter is designed to develop market judgment by observation of past market actions. We have set down here lists of those issues on the New York Stock Exchange (NYSE) and the American Stock Exchange (AMEX) that doubled in the years 1962 through 1964. The purpose of listing winners in these years is (1) to highlight the kinds of stock that can score important gains, and (2) to note that, in certain years, gainful speculation is quite difficult. For example, 1962 was a year of across-the-board declines on both exchanges. Net advances were rare oases in a downward spiral. Had we sought to double our money in that year, the best way would have been to sell short — or to follow Billy Rose's advice about doubling your money: take it out of your pocket, fold it over once, and then put it back in your pocket.

1962 NYSE DOUBLERS

STOCK	FIRST SALE OF YEAR	LAST SALE OF YEAR
Consolidated Cigar	21 7/8 adj. for 3-for-1 split	49 3/4

1962 AMEX DOUBLERS

STOCK	FIRST SALE OF YEAR	LAST SALE OF YEAR
Simca Automobiles	16	44 1/2 (bid)

1963 NYSE DOUBLERS

STOCK	FIRST SALE OF YEAR	LAST SALE OF YEAR
Bulova Watch	9 7/8	26
Chicago & North Western	13 1/4	25 1/2 (almost)
Chrysler	18 3/8 adj. price. Chrysler had two 2-for-1 splits in 1963.	42
Dr. Pepper	21 1/2 (bid)	49 7/8
Evans Products	9 1/2	20 1/8
Haveg Industries	19 7/8	39 (almost)
Monon Railroad, Class B	9 3/8	29 7/8
Northwest Airlines	37 7/8	73 1/2
Pan American World Airways	21 3/8	52 1/2
St. Joseph Lead	25 1/4	51 1/4
Shahmoon Industries	9 1/2	19 1/2
Western Air Lines	31 3/4	73
Xerox	31 1/4 adj. for 5-for-1 split.	85

1963 AMEX DOUBLERS

STOCK	FIRST SALE OF YEAR	LAST SALE OF YEAR
Atlas Consolidated Mining & Development	6 7/8	14 5/8
Bunker Hill	8 3/4	22 1/2
Carey Baxter & Kennedy	4 (bid)	9
Dennison Manufacturing, Class A	19	54 1/4
Falcon Seaboard Drilling	4 3/8 (bid)	14 1/2
Felmont Oil	5 1/4	10 3/8 (almost)
Guerdon Industries	3 1/2	7 5/8
Gulf States Land & Industries	14 3/4	28 3/4
Kin-Ark Oil	1 5/8	4 1/8
Mount Clemens Metal Products	5 7/8	13 7/8
New Process	38 7/8	80 1/2
Philips Electronics & Pharmaceuticals	25	55 3/8
Pyle National	26 1/8	65 3/4
Rayette	23 1/4	46 (almost)
San Carlos Milling	7 1/4 (bid)	14 (almost)
Silicon Transistor	4 3/8	11
Syntex	12 adj. for 3-for-1 split.	125
Technicolor	8 3/4	18 5/8
Zapata Off-Shore	4 3/4 (bid)	9 7/8

1964 NYSE DOUBLERS

STOCK	FIRST SALE OF YEAR	LAST SALE OF YEAR
Braniff Airways	13	27 3/4
Bucyrus-Erie	19 5/8	39 3/8
Chicago & North Western	25 7/8	57 7/8
Evans Products	21 5/8	42 3/4
Fluor	16	35
I-T-E Circuit Breaker	17 1/2	38

STOCK	FIRST SALE OF YEAR	LAST SALE OF YEAR
Pan American Sulphur	20 3/4	44 7/8
Sunshine Mining	10 7/8	25 3/8
Texas Gulf Sulphur	24 1/8	51 1/8

1964 AMEX DOUBLERS

STOCK	FIRST SALE OF YEAR	LAST SALE OF YEAR
Acme Missiles & Construction	2	7 1/4
Aeronca	2 1/4	6 1/8
Allied Paper	6 3/4	13 7/8
Alloys Unlimited	4 3/8	13 1/8
APL	5 1/4	11 1/8
Berkey Photo	9 1/2	19 3/8
Brazilian Traction (now Brazilian Light & Power)	2 3/8	4 7/8
Data-Control Systems	24 1/2	56 1/4
Day Mines	5 1/8	10 3/4
Driver-Harris	17 1/2 (bid)	35 1/2
Fotochrome	2	9 1/4
Fresnillo	6 3/4	13 5/8
Greer Hydraulics	2 1/2	12 1/8
Holly	9 1/4	23
International Products	3 7/8	15 1/4
D. Kaltman	1 3/8	4 1/2
Kin-Ark Oil	4 1/4	9 1/4
Lee Filter	2	5 1/8
Magellan Petroleum	13/16	4
Missouri-Kansas-Texas certificates	5	15 1/8
Norfolk Southern	12 1/2	30
Old Town	8 3/8	38 3/8
Pantasote	3 1/4	7
Rollins	16 3/4	76 1/4
Savoy Industries	8 3/4	30
Unexcelled	6 3/4	26 1/4
Unishops	9 3/4	21 1/8

1962

This year, as you can see, was a dreary one for avid traders, and had this book come out in June, 1962, it would have languished. In midsummer of that year, people weren't very confident that any stock could ever double; and only two actually did.

1963

The year 1963 was a rebound year. Sentiment, which was so gloomy in mid-1962 (after the market had fallen 30 percent in six months), turned confident, and many issues rose not so much because of notable advances in earning power as because they had been hammered down below their worth a year earlier. The lively uptick was far more visible on AMEX than on the Big Board, however. On the NYSE, the sensational performers were two rails (Chicago & North West and Monon Railroad, Class B) and three airlines (Pan American, Northwest, and Western). Xerox Corporation, one of the few stocks to be a market darling for several years in a row, attained virtuosity in 1963. In Xerox, the propellants were the dynamics of the copy-machine industry and the solid industrial leadership and rapid rise in earnings of the company (accompanied by stock splits); and significant buying by certain institutions.

On AMEX, the year 1963 turned the spotlight of interest onto offshore oil drilling, with 100 percent gains by Falcon Seaboard and Zapata Off-Shore. Metals were favored, too. Atlas Consolidated and Bunker Hill moved ahead in price, and both companies gained notably in corporate stature. Other issues scored well in response to substantial growth in earning power: Rayette, Dennison Manufacturing, and New Process Company. Finally, Syntex moved sensationally, reporting a tenfold gain—a stock with definite sex appeal.

1964

During 1964, there was no market basket full of winners on the NYSE — only nine. They included an airline,
Braniff; two construction-industry entries, Bucyrus-Erie
and Fluor Corporation; a volatile industrial, Evans Products; Sunshine Mining, with a silver lining; and Texas
Gulf Sulphur, which had a mixed blessing (SEC investigation) in its big copper strike at Timmins, Ontario.

The list of double gainers on AMEX was substantial —
twenty-seven. Stellar performers were Brazilian Traction,
the billion-dollar electric-light-and-power company in
Brazil; Data-Control Systems, a leader in automation;
Magellan Petroleum, scoring on an oil strike in Australia;
and technical companies — Acme Missiles, Greer Hydraulics, Lee Filter, Alloys Unlimited, and Unexcelled, Inc.
Two railroads made the scene — Norfolk Southern and
Missouri-Kansas-Texas certificates. This seemed to be
a year for special speculative situations, and on AMEX,
shares that performed best had rather small capitalizations and thin floating supplies in the market (Alloys,
Norfolk Southern, Greer Hydraulics).

The years 1962-64 illustrate our thesis quite well. In
years when markets are strong, a significant number of
stocks will double in value. Unusual increases in per
share earnings are the most common and dependable
motivating forces. Equally, in bear or depressed markets,
even issues with very good earnings and golden prospects
have a hard time bucking the tide, and doublers are few.

14

big swings in 1965 and 1966

The New York Stock Exchange lists about 1,240 issues of common stock, and these include the equities of some of the largest, most famous companies in the world. There is AT&T, with 541 million shares of stock outstanding; General Motors, with 286 million; and other giant blue chips such as U.S. Steel, Sears, Roebuck, Standard Oil of New Jersey, Texaco, Swift & Company, and Pacific Gas & Electric. But the shares of titanic enterprises, as you will note from the tabulations that follow, while trading in great volume, are seldom dazzling performers or dramatic movers within any short period of time. In fact, in our search for annual doublers, we must almost rule out the shares of the two hundred largest corporations.

It's uncommon for any one of them to move widely in a hurry, first, because they have so many millions of shares outstanding and, second, because they already have such huge earnings that it would be most unusual for one of them to increase its net profits within a single year by as much as 50 percent. (Rising earnings, or the expectations of them, are the most powerful underlying market propellants.) So the first principle we can set down in advance is this: If you seek a 100 percent gain within a year, don't buy shares in the biggest companies. Look over the feature gainers for 1965 and you'll see that it's among the second and third echelons of companies that the biggest swings on the Big Board occur.

The year 1965 was a fine and representative bull-market year, in which there were fifty-five issues on the New York Stock Exchange that doubled. Our definition of a doubler, in any year, is a stock that on the last trading day of the subject year was selling at least twice as high as it sold on the first business day in January. Actually, this arbitrarily restricts the list, because a number of stocks that do not qualify on this basis actually doubled in price some time during the year but were unable to hold their gain until the year end.

In any event, 1965 was an excellent year in which to test our theories. Here is the list of January-to-December doublers, with comment on the group and certain individual performances following directly thereafter:

1965 NYSE DOUBLERS

STOCK	FIRST SALE OF YEAR	LAST SALE OF YEAR
Admiral Corporation	15 3/4	65
Allied Products	10 1/4	35
American Ship Building	13	26 1/4
Bangor Punta Alegre Sugar	15 1/8	32 1/2

STOCK	FIRST SALE OF YEAR	LAST SALE OF YEAR
Boston & Maine	10 1/2	23 3/4
Braniff Airways	27 5/8	72 7/8
Burndy	15 5/8	46
Burroughs Corporation	25	49 7/8
Chemetron	27 1/4	57 7/8
Chicago & North Western	58 1/2	121
Collins Radio	19 1/2	49 1/4
Colt Industries	12	23 5/8
Congoleum-Nairn	15 1/2	35 7/8
Consolidated Freightways (moved from OTC during year)	19 1/2 (OTC)	44 1/4
Continental Air Lines	20	52 7/8
Continental Copper & Steel	7 7/8	22 3/4
Crescent	10 1/8	19 7/8
CTS	25 7/8	59
Delta Air Lines	30 7/8 adj. figure. Split 2 for 1 Nov.	71 1/2
Douglas Aircraft	29 1/4	74 5/8
Eastern Air Lines	42 1/2	89
Emerson Radio & Phonograph	10 3/8	22
Fairchild Camera & Instrument	27 3/4	150 1/2
Fairchild Hiller	9 1/8	18
Fansteel Metallurgical	10 3/8	20 1/8
Gulf & Western Industries	31 1/2	92 7/8
Holiday Inns of America	16 3/8	31 5/8
International Rectifier	7 1/4	18 1/8
IRC	14 1/8	29 5/8
Lehigh Valley Industries	2 1/4	8 1/4
Ling-Temco-Vought	17 3/4	48 1/4
Litton Industries	74 7/8 split 2 for 1 Dec. Old common shown.	139
Lukens Steel	20 5/8 split 2 for 1 Dec. Old common shown.	53 1/8
Magnavox	31 3/4	81 7/8
Motorola	95 1/2	164 1/2
National Airlines	34 adj. 2-for-1 split	70 1/4

STOCK	FIRST SALE OF YEAR	LAST SALE OF YEAR
New Jersey Zinc	23	49
Northwest Airlines	63 1/4	127 5/8
Pittsburgh Coke & Chemical	20 1/2	49 1/8
Polaroid	45 7/8	116 5/8
Rohr	18 7/8	42 1/4
Ryan Aeronautical	9 1/16	17 3/4
	adj. 2-for-1 split	
Sangamo Electric	10 3/8	30
SCM	17 1/2	53 1/2
Spartans Industries	16 3/4	39 1/2
Standard Kollsman Industries	8 5/8	23 1/8
Union Carbide	29 3/8	68 1/2
	adj. 3-for-1 split	
United Aircraft Corporation	21 7/8	82 1/8
Varian Associates	13 1/8	26 5/8
Victor Comptometer	15 3/8	33 1/2
Vornado	30 3/8	68 3/4
Ward Foods	6 7/8	16 3/4
White Consolidated Industries	18	48 3/4
Xerox	99	202
Zenith Radio	63 1/2	121 1/4

COMMENT ON 1965 NYSE DOUBLERS

The year 1965 was a flowering one for speculators on the NYSE. There were fifty-five doublers and they appeared in almost every category. First of all, the year was a general boom year — in motorcars, construction, merchandising, utilities, finance, metals, mining, rails, airlines, and Gross National Product. The year seemed a safe and promising one, and more stockholders and speculators were on the scene than at any time in history. It was thus to be expected that trader confidence was bubbling, and that speculation would spread across the Board to include almost any stock of merit and motion. Also, many issues traded in probably greater volume than ever before — Eastern Air Lines, Chicago & North West, Fairchild Camera, Polaroid, Motorola, SCM, and Admiral, for example. This was the year of the "performance" stocks — issues with wide popular appeal and notable rises in earnings that attracted heavy mutual-fund buying for speculative gain. The point was brought forcibly home that stocks could swing lustily up and down from day to day, with these swings quite unaccounted for by any specific improvement or deterioration in the welfare of the subject companies.

In substantial companies with a popular appeal, such as SCM, Xerox, Syntex, supply-demand factors seemed to dictate price changes. Issues with the smallest floating supplies frequently performed best, and several stocks were pushed up simply because buyers day after day outnumbered sellers. Add to this built-up individual clamor for particular issues the frequent buy orders, in 5,000 to 50,000 lots, by the funds, and you can understand how there developed a mass-market psychology that was roaringly bullish, and that carried many issues to alpine levels found to be quite untenable a year later.

The list of NYSE 1965 leaders should be studied quite carefully by speculators. In particular, it would be useful to look up the percentage of outstanding shares of an issue traded in the course of a year. It is an observable phenomenon in bull markets that sharp increase in volume in an active issue is usually accompanied by rising prices. For this reason, many successful speculators watch the volume of trading in individual issues like hawks, and when they see a stock *suddenly trading in twice its accustomed volume and rising on this volume, they buy.* They do so often without bothering to look up the fundamental data — earnings, dividends, profit margins, growth rates, etc. Such traders believe the secret of market success lies in riding stock trends rather than depending on improved earnings to be slowly reflected in the price of a stock, which has attracted no eager group of followers.

The year also illustrated another important point useful for speculators — the advantage of trading in "hot" industries. In 1965, nearly all analysts, economists, and investment services were convinced that air transportation had come of age; that the high costs of converting from "props" to jets had been assimilated; and that airlines would now make money as they began to fill all the new seating capacity acquired. Speculators throughout the land "bought" this theory of airline prosperity — and look at the stock gains that resulted in a single year! Braniff, Continental, Delta, Eastern, National, Northwest — all more than doubled, with a related gain in United Aircraft, largest builder of jet engines.

Following further this "popular industry" theory, look at TV in 1965! People were convinced that color TV was about to really "take over," so traders swarmed all over Admiral (which quadrupled in price), Collins, Emerson, Magnavox, Motorola, and Zenith. Just think of this: if, in January, 1965, you had become convinced that only two industries were then worth speculating in, and forthwith purchased all the TV and airline issues cited in the previous paragraphs, you would have owned twelve stocks that doubled — and nobody could have done better than that! So start now picking the "hot" industry for 1968-69.

While the foregoing group of dramatic gainers is just what the doctor ordered for our purposes, note that these fifty-five issues that doubled are only 4.5 percent of all the issues listed on the NYSE. Also, observe that the Dow-Jones Industrial Average — the most famous market barometer — displayed an average rise of only 10.88 percent for the full year. The issues on this list thus represent an elite group. In some way, and for a variety of reasons, this small list of stocks outperformed the whole market by a very wide margin. Let's try to see why some of these virtuosos performed so well, not as an historical exercise, but to observe from these standouts the particular qualities they possessed that made them so eagerly sought and bought. Are there certain vital ingredients common to all hot stocks? We think so.

POLAROID CORPORATION

Here's an obvious swinger! Widely talked about in board rooms from coast to coast, it qualifies as a "hot stock" by having risen in 1965 from a low of 44 to a high of 130. Possibly one of the reasons for the "action" was the very name of one of its leading products, the Swinger camera! Over 800,000 Model 20's were sold in 1965; and treble that in 1966.

Polaroid, renowned for excellence in instant and color photography, offered many facets of attraction to speculators: (1) the popularity of photography in a high-leisure, high-income society; (2) the lure of Polaroid's almost continuous improvements; (3) the rapid advance in earnings, from 71 cents in 1963 to more than double that in 1965; (4) the steady "repeat" demand for film; (5) whispers about an exciting new TV tube and a novel copying machine; and (6) a pretax profit margin of above 27 percent.

It is hard to decide which of the foregoing plus factors were most influential in causing Polaroid to go up. It is to be observed, however, that together these elements produced a picture of profits, progress, and potential about Polaroid so attractive that, after drifting in lower price zones for four years, the stock broke away in 1965 and rewarded early buyers with market gains of well over 100 percent. This is an exciting picture, whether viewed from a slide rule or from a Polaroid lens. Finally, market motion was stimulated by belief that Polaroid would increase its sales by 30 percent-plus in 1966. It did! Polaroid in 1965 was a classic study in glamour and gain, with its stock undulating in a broad market terrain provided by 15,750,000 shares listed and traded on the NYSE.

NORTHWEST AIRLINES, INC.

This proved a most rewarding selection in 1965, moving from a low of 61¾ to a high of 142½ (and still higher in 1966). What was the propulsion here? (1) A widely held belief that air transportation had come of age and that a long-term uptrend in traffic revenues and profits was now discernible; (2) the fact that Northwest was an elite selection within the industry on the basis of historic growth, excellence of management, taut cost controls, an ultramodern jet fleet, and some of the most desirable air routes in the world; (3) the upthrust in earnings from $5.86 a share in 1964 to an indicated $10 in 1965 and possibly $13 in 1966; and (4) the probability of higher dividends and a stock split.

The combination of these factors generated a powerful market following in NWA even though the stock orbited in a price range not generally popular. A review and acceptance of the four points listed above early in 1965 would have provided ample justification for speculative purchase, especially because the whole airline group documented its popularity by heavy trading profits and exciting gains in other issues — Eastern, Braniff, National, Pan Am, etc. The real logic behind the purchase of NWA was that it was probably the choicest major stock in a surging industry. Perhaps it still is.

SCM CORPORATION

Here was a real breakaway stock in 1965. Under its pre-1958 name of Smith-Corona Marchant, Inc., the company had turned in rather routine earnings and so-so market performance for a few years, when suddenly it "caught on." The company, benefiting from vigorous topside direction under Mr. Emerson B. Mead, President, increased its sales by over 60 percent in six years, and in two years' time became the second largest producer (next to Xerox) of electrostatic copiers; and the only maker of electric portable typewriters. Plant capacity was greatly increased, and production costs significantly reduced by automation.

These elements were all important, but the clincher was the resultant sharp rise in earnings for fiscal 1965 (year ending June 30). Net income per share rose 57 percent to $1.47, against 83 cents a share in 1964. Because of the glamour of the business-machine industry, generated and sustained by IBM and Xerox, and SCM's dramatic advances within the industry in sales and profits, this stock became a hot one. Its earlier rise from 10½ to over 20 in 1963-64 set the base and provided the launching pad for a driving gain in 1965, from a low of 16¼ to a high of 62⅝ (well over 300 percent). During the year, 11,106,000 shares of SCM were traded — about four times its capitalization. Such a volume of trading, on the upside, is a usual characteristic of a breakaway stock.

ADMIRAL CORPORATION

One of the explosive industries of 1965 was color TV. After a decade of research, color tubes were improved, and new color sets, offered at somewhat lower prices, caught on big. Projections for 1965 indicated that, by the year's end, there would be 55 million homes with TV sets, but only 5.4 million with color sets. This pointed to a fantastic demand for future years, as color-TV ownership became a social compulsion, and as programs in color expanded to satisfy viewers and advertisers alike.

Color consoles thus became the "in" thing, in both suburbia and Wall Street, and the shares of the standout producers became market darlings. There was a surging board-room clamor for Zenith, Motorola, RCA, and Magnavox, but no issue generated a more ecstatic following than Admiral. It rose during the year from 16 to 56, although it paid no dividend; and it continued its spectacular rise well into 1966. Why was this? What were the propulsive forces behind Admiral? Sales and earnings, basically.

First-half sales in 1965 at Admiral were up 32 percent, and net earnings 61 percent! Sales, which were $238 million for the full year 1964, were expected to cross $280 million in 1965 (they did); and net earnings were expected to rise from $1.66 (1964) to above $2.50, and this after heavy charge-offs ($1 a share pretax) for entering color-tube manufacture. Admiral, which had been buying its spectrum tubes principally from National Video and Sylvania, decided to manufacture its own 25-inch color tubes beginning in 1965, and added 19-inch tubes in 1966. This was to ensure adequate supply and prompt deliveries, and incidentally to improve overall manufacturing profitability.

Altogether, Admiral appeared on the threshold of dramatic gains in sales and profits running well into future years. There were unofficial estimates that Admiral might even duplicate its 1950 results, when the company earned $7.67 (prior to which the stock had also advanced several hundred percent).

Thus, in review, Admiral became a hot stock in 1965 because: (1) the company was astride the mainstream of consumer electronic demand — color TV; (2) it was producing attractive sets with increasing profit margins; (3) it was creating its own color-tube facility; (4) net profits might treble within three years; and (5) the company had a small capitalization (only 2,450,000 shares) with 40 percent owned by management, which resulted in a small floating supply of shares, always a powerful

market force in hot stocks. Finally, there was the linger-
ing memory, among older traders, of swift and extraordi-
nary gains in Admiral in the 1948-50 period. Admiral is
a copybook example of hot stock. (It was no longer such
in 1967-68.)

FAIRCHILD CAMERA & INSTRUMENT CORPORATION

The largest percentage rise in 1965 in any company
shares listed on the Big Board was scored by Fairchild
Camera. From 27½ at the end of 1964, the stock closed in
1965 at 150½, an advance of 447.3 percent. This standout performance may be attributed to four things: (1)
romance, (2) a dazzling rise in sales and earnings, (3)
a remarkable improvement in pretax margins, and (4) a
relatively small share capitalization.

The romance was provided by Fairchild's leadership
in the electronic field of integrated microcircuits; its
cockpit voice recorder, now required on all jet aircraft;
and its significant position in space and defense systems.

Early in 1965, analysts were convinced that Fairchild
would surge ahead statistically—and it surely lived up
to its billing. Sales rose 30 percent above 1964, and net
earnings advanced dramatically from 75 cents (1964) to
$3.25 in 1965. Pretax profit margins—2.6 percent in the
earlier year—were 9 percent in 1965, an impressive improvement and solid evidence of managerial excellence.

Capitalization (December 31, 1964) was $29.7 million in
long-term debt, followed by only 2,556,657 shares of common. Proving the popularity of this stock, 10,017,900
shares changed hands in 1965—four times the outstanding capital! When you see such volume in trading,
on the up side in relation to shares outstanding, you almost certainly mark a hot stock with almost compulsive
forward momentum. Earning projection for Fairchild for

1966 was over $5 a share, an excellent gain also, but not enough to make Fairchild common advance another 400 percent! Fairchild in 1965 had everything going for it!

Concluding our NYSE observations on 1965, the year was notable for its industry preferences, with airlines and TV hogging the spotlight. The year further illustrates the influence of institutional buying of glamour and action stocks. In prior years, mutual funds were generally regarded as conservative acquirers of seasoned equities for long-term investment. In 1965, however, institutional investors on the average turned over 21 percent of their portfolios. This indicated that many funds had become heavy in-and-out traders in the market. Some funds indeed gained a reputation for "performance," and the securities they bought (when that information became available) were carefully noted and frequently bought also by shrewd individual traders. This big-volume buying by funds and active traders was important in carrying certain of the above issues to their highs in 1965. Equally, however, liquidation of certain issues by funds in 1967-68 set in motion a chain of liquidation orders. Thus institutional action on the selling side can become a powerful actual and psychological market depressant. We can hardly expect to find a stock that is likely to double swiftly among those issues being sold by funds, especially by those with notable records of prior success in market trading. For guidance in your own speculative decisions about the more actively traded and popular issues, it may be very useful for you to watch what the funds are doing. They are not always right, but their decisions are made by trained market professionals, with their reputations, and sometimes their jobs, depending on their evaluations of securities and trends. The funds in fact create trends for issues, but speculators should be alert to liquidate before the funds do!

AMEX: SMALLER ISSUES, THINNER MARKETS

Our avowed goal is swift capital gain; and in our cease-less quest for this, we are far more interested in potential market velocity than in intrinsic investment quality. From this viewpoint, the approximately 1,050 issues on the American Stock Exchange offer a more fertile hunting ground for speculation than does the Big Board. This is true for several reasons.

American Exchange listings are generally of much smaller companies, often in an early development stage and growing at much faster rates than the corporate giants on the New York Stock Exchange. To illustrate, on February 1, 1966, the average market value per issue of stocks listed on AMEX was about $27 million, against an average value per issue on the NYSE of roughly $420 million. On the same date, the trading price of the average AMEX issue was about $18 a share, against approximately $50 for shares on the NYSE. Lower price ranges invariably attract more speculators and generate more extensive and more animated trading activity. However, probably the most important factor responsible for the dazzling trading swings which occur on AMEX is small average capitalization. On the Big Board, at least 700,000 outstanding shares held by the public are required for listing. The AMEX minimum is only 250,000 shares, and in many issues the floating supply is amazingly thin. In such instances, an order to buy as little as 2,000 shares of a stock selling at $5 can move the market up half a point or more (10 percent). This action, reported in the papers, may attract the attention of speculators and inject heavy buying power into an issue already very thin on the offering side — and the market may start an upward surge aided and abetted by scarcity of offerings. On any average trading day on AMEX, you can observe many issues in which the total trading volume does not exceed $5,000.

Just a little extra volume—whether buying or selling—can stimulate erratic price swings in such issues.

Because they sell in lower price ranges, stocks on AMEX are more prone to double than higher-price shares on the Big Board. A stock selling at 5 is more than twice as likely to double in a given time interval than one at 50. Further, since the average AMEX issue has far fewer shares outstanding, aggressive buying can stimulate swift price rises due to relative scarcity of the stock in question.

Other factors conducive to wider percentage swings on the American Stock Exchange are: (1) AMEX issues are usually of younger companies, often growing at faster rates than their brethren on the NYSE; (2) trading by individuals accounts for a larger percentage of total volume, over 50 percent, on AMEX, accompanied by less institutional buying than on the Big Board, since institutional buying as a rule is much less speculative in character.

With this short reference to the more energized and bouncy trading climate on AMEX, we present that exchange's Hit Parade for 1965: altogether, 104 stocks that advanced by at least 100 percent in value.

1965 AMEX DOUBLERS

STOCK	FIRST SALE OF YEAR	LAST SALE OF YEAR
Allegheny Airlines	4 3/8	13
Allied Control	7 1/8	24 5/8
Alloys Unlimited	13 1/8	46
American Beverage	3 1/2	9 3/8
American Book Company	10 7/8	23 7/8
American Electronics	1	2 3/8
American Safety Equipment	5 1/4	13
Andrea Radio	7 5/8	24
Argus	3 1/4	8 3/4

STOCK	FIRST SALE OF YEAR	LAST SALE OF YEAR
Asamera Oil	5/8	2 1/2
Astrex	2 1/4	6 3/8
Audio Devices	8 1/8	22 5/8
Automatic Radio	2 1/8	4 5/8
Avien	1/2	3 1/2
Banff Oil	1 1/8	7 1/4
Bell Electronics	1 7/8	5
Berkey Photo (moved to NYSE during year)	19 3/8	39 1/8
Bowling Corporation of America	1 3/8	2 3/4
Bowser	5 1/2	12
Caldor	10 1/4	23 1/2
CCI	1 1/2	3 5/8
Century Geophysical	2 5/8	10 3/4
Chief Consolidated Mining	2 5/8	5 5/8
Chromalloy American	15 5/8	35 5/8
Clarostat Manufacturing	5 5/8	11 3/8
Computer Sciences	7 3/4	21 5/8
Condec	4 7/8	10 1/4
Continental Aviation	8	16 1/2
Cubic	4 7/8	10 3/4
Dixilyn	2 1/2	9 1/8
Duraloy	2 1/8	6 3/8
Dynalectron	3	6 5/8
Eastern Air Devices	3/4	6 3/4
Eckerd Drugs (Florida)	12 1/2	26
Elco	10 1/4	23
Electro-Voice	5 1/2	17 1/8
Electronic Communications	8 1/2	17 7/8
Espey Manufacturing & Electronics	4	9 7/8
M. H. Fishman	10 1/8	24 7/8
Flying Tiger Line	9 1/2	28 1/4
Frontier Airlines	8 1/8	18 5/8
General Alloys	2 5/8	6
A. C. Gilbert	9 1/4	20 3/8
Gordon Jewelry	13 1/2	34 1/4
GTI	3 1/8	9 1/4
Gulf American	4 7/8	10 1/4
H & B American	3 3/8	6 3/4

STOCK	FIRST SALE OF YEAR	LAST SALE OF YEAR
C. M. Hall Lamp	2 3/4	11 1/2
R. Hoe	3	6 7/8
Philip A. Hunt Chemical	12 3/4	29 1/8
Hycon	6 3/4	15 7/8
IMC Magnetics	3 1/8	6 3/8
Jefferson Lake Petrochemicals	9 1/16	22 1/2
Walter Kidde	16	45 3/4
Lee Motor Products	1 1/4	2 1/2
Lockwood, Kessler & Bartlett	2 1/8	8 3/4
Lundy Electronics & Systems	6 1/4	16 3/4
Mallory Randall	1 3/4	5
Maul Brothers	4 1/4	11 1/4
Microwave Associates	9 5/8	21 1/2
Mohawk Airlines	6 1/4	16 3/4
Monogram Industries	7	15 7/8
Morse Electro Products	1	2 3/8
National Video	8 3/8	83 1/2
Northeast Airlines	4 1/2	31 5/8
Pacific Northern Airlines	3 3/4	14 1/2
Pioneer Aerodynamic Systems	3	10 1/8
Planning Research	12	34
Pneumo Dynamics	16 7/8	42 1/4
Poloron Products	2 1/4	6
Potter Instrument	6 3/4	16
Robinson Technical Products	3 3/4	8 3/8
Rodney Metals	4 1/2	9
Rowland Products	8 3/4	34 1/4
Royal American Industries	11/16	1 1/2
Ryan Consolidated Petroleum	2 7/8	6 3/8
Seaboard World Airlines	6	14
Sealectro	4 3/8	9 1/4
Seeman Brothers	4 1/8	9
Sel-Rex	11 5/8	24 3/4
Simmonds Precision Products	7 3/4	56 1/2
Slick	5 1/4	11 1/2
Solitron Devices	39 1/2	132 1/4
Soss Manufacturing	9 1/4	19 3/8
Southern Realty & Utilities	1	3 1/2
Speed-O-Print Business Machines	7 1/8	15 7/8

STOCK	FIRST SALE OF YEAR	LAST SALE OF YEAR
Stanley Aviation	4	10 3/4
Statham Instruments	14 5/8	29 3/8
Sunair Electronics	2	4 3/8
Supronics	1 1/8	2 3/4
Syntex	32 7/8	97 7/8
Technical Operations	19 1/2	47 1/4
Teleprompter	6 7/8	19 1/4
Television Industries	5/8	2
Tenney Engineering	1 3/4	4
Terminal-Hudson Electronics	2 1/4	6
Thompson-Starrett	1 1/4	5 7/8
Universal Automated Industries	9/16	3 1/2
Weiman	5 3/4	15 5/8
Western Equities	7 5/8	42 7/8
Western Nuclear	5 1/4	14
Wieboldt Stores	6 5/8	17
Williamhouse	7 5/8	15 1/2
XTRA	9 1/8	51

Here indeed is excellent proof that we are on the right track. There are plenty of stocks that can double in a year. Almost one stock out of every ten on AMEX *doubled in 1965*; and a number of these recorded far greater gains. Altogether, twelve of the above advanced between 200 and 300 percent; five advanced 300 to 400 percent; two 400 to 500 percent; and five stocks (Avien, Eastern Air Devices, National Video, Northeast Airlines, and Simmonds Precision Products) delighted their holders by gaining over 500 percent! The champ was National Video, which grew by almost 900 percent (but by 1968 its glamour had all worn off).

WHAT PUSHED THEM UP?

It would be nice to think that all these gains were logical and impelled by such fundamental forces as dramatic improvement in earnings or rising dividend payments; but these propulsive forces are notably absent. Take Avien, a little aircraft-supply company making no money but rather suspended in that twilight zone of solvency, Chapter XI of the Bankruptcy Act. New capital was located for this troubled company, and Avien shares responded by leaping from 50 cents to $3.50; and 70 percent of Avien capitalization of 1,370,000 shares turned over during the year.

Northeast Airlines is another trader's darling that made the grade without benefit of earnings. The company had been losing money for several years but got a new lease on life when it was granted a license to run from Boston and New York to Miami. The other lines weren't exactly crazy about this, and attempts were made to eliminate Northeast from this lucrative run. But the license was retained; some new planes were added; and, most important, in 1965 Storer Broadcasting Company gained control by buying a block of Northeast at around $5 a share. That's all that was needed. In the most favorable market climate for airlines since 1946, Northeast took off with a tail wind, gaining 600 percent altitude for the year. Other airline issues sparkling on AMEX in 1965 included Allegheny, Continental Aviation, Flying Tiger, Frontier, Mohawk, Pacific Northern, and Seaboard World. It was a great year to be airborne in the market!

Banff Oil shows what can happen when the drill bit hits the right oilfield. Banff was just an ordinary little "penny" Canadian company, a small producer, when early in 1965 it made a rich crude discovery at appropriately named Rainbow Lake in northwest Alberta. Banff was the operator on a sizable chunk of oil-prone terrain — over 46,000 lease acres. Banff had some strong partners, too — Aquitaine Company, owned by the huge French government oil complex, and Mobil Oil. Out of the first ten wells drilled, six were successful, and an oilfield with reserves of possibly 600 million barrels was indicated. On the strength of this strike, a 240-mile, 20-inch pipeline was immediately planned to run from Rainbow to Nisipi.

While Banff's interest in Rainbow Lake is only 5 percent (Aquitaine has 45 percent and Mobil 50 percent), Banff also has a royalty interest in a gas field at Gold Lake worth around $10 million at the 1965 year end. With all this, Banff earned only 1 cent a share in 1964, before the fireworks began. The stock gained 500 percent in 1965, and doubled again in 1966. Trading for 1965 was about 4 million shares — almost a 100 percent turnover of its 4,215,000 outstanding shares. Banff, listed on both AMEX and Toronto, has been a lively performer and appears to have a lot of speculative oomph still left even after its dazzling series of rises.

Accompanying Banff on the Hit Parade of oils were: Asamera, Jefferson Lake, and Ryan Consolidated.

COLOR TV

As we saw on the NYSE, Admiral and Motorola gained soaringly. Color TV shares were just as fashionable and animate on AMEX. National Video showed the way.

National Video, in 1965, was the fourth largest color-TV-tube manufacturer (after RCA, Zenith, and Sylvania). It had had no impressive track record. The stock sold at 3 in 1963 and closed at 8⅜ in 1964. It earned but 10 cents a share in fiscal 1965 (year ending May 31). Then its sales began to pick up, trebling to an annual rate of around $75 million; profits improved ($1.14 for the half year ending November 30, 1965); and the stock gained an irrepressible following, closing the year at 83½, with lots of drive left over for 1966. Just how a stock so specialized and so dependent on a single competitive product deserved to gain such market altitude is a little hard to see. Others — Motorola, Sylvania, and Admiral — expanded their color-tube production in 1965. Did National Video really justify

a market valuation of over $200 at the 1965 year end?
Earnings were rising—but that much? Despite these
queries, the stock gained fabulously, which is all we can
ask of any stock. At least temporarily.

At the tail of the color-TV-market comet were a couple
of other AMEX swingers, Thompson-Starrett and Noramco. Thompson-Starrett not only doubled but actually
gained 370 percent for the year. Its full range was between 1 and 9¼. T-S is in reality a building-construction
firm with a subsidiary making TV and radio sets. Rumor
had it that T-S had come upon a notable technical advance in color TV and the stock shot up like a Titan rocket.
As it turned out, the stock earned only 10 cents a share
for calendar 1965, and the TV virtuosity was greatly over-
played. Here again the reasons for such a rise were mostly
psychological and had little reference to earning power.

Honorable mention is probably due Noramco, which
doubled during the year even though it couldn't hold its
gains. Noramco's main business is the Dugan Bakery
division, a door-to-door bakery company; but a Wall Street
rumor had it that the company had the patent rights to a
revolutionary new flat color-TV tube. The sheep flocked
in and bought Noramco heavily against a total 1.5 million
share capitalization; and the stock zoomed from 3 to 10
within thirty days. It swiftly "fell out of bed," however,
after the SEC suspended trading in the issue. The color
TV "breakthrough" was apparently pretty nebulous. In
due course, after all that market hoopla, Noramco showed
a loss in 1965—as it had for several earlier years. Another illustration of market gains synthetically induced.
And in 1966, Noramco was in Chapter XI of the Bankruptcy Act.

Further documenting the fact that market leaders in
1965 were heavily concentrated in a few industries, note
the roster of electronic performers above: Audio Devices,
Automatic Radio, Bell Electronics, Dynalectron, Elec-

tronic Communications, Hycon, IMC Magnetics, Lundy Electronics, Microwave Associates, Potter Instrument, Solitron (the most magnificent), Sunair Electronics, Supronics, Television Industries, and Terminal-Hudson, which has since been placed under investigation. In general summary, it is worth noting that in 1965, fifty stocks of those doubling on AMEX *started their moves below $5 a share!* This powerfully emphasizes the fact that shares in the $5 or less zone are the best ones to look at to find happiness in stocks that double. The greater the risk, the greater the possible reward.

1966 DOUBLERS

Having reviewed a year — 1965 — in which speculation for fun and profit was rampant, we come next to the sobering-up period. In 1966, the DJIA declined 19.8 percent for the year, and the NYSE dipped 20 percent. It took a real virtuoso to double between January and December. In fact, we had to stretch a bit to come up with three!

1966 NYSE DOUBLERS

STOCK	FIRST SALE OF YEAR	LAST SALE OF YEAR
American Research & Development	20 1/4	40 (almost)
Braniff Airways	36 3/8	70 (almost)
Howmet	20 3/8	48 1/4

Here the explanations are simple. American Research invests in young companies and provides guidance in their development into profitable and successful enterprises. In 1966, one of the companies it had invested in and sponsored, Digital Equipment, made great strides and its stock gained greatly in value. This gain was reflected in ARD.

Howmet (formerly Howe Sound Company) moved up on notable gains in earnings. Braniff reflected excellent advance in earnings and the market leverage created by a rather small floating supply of stock, with about 80 percent of the common held by Greatamerica Corporation.

We can, in fact, glean little from NYSE market action in 1966, except to observe once again that the favorable climate provided by a bull market is most essential if you seek stocks that double in a year. Even companies with earnings advancing spectacularly have a tough time swimming against the tide of a bear market, and 1966 was a bear year!

AMEX got the message, too, and declined in a similar manner. On the American Stock Exchange, the doublers were:

1966 AMEX DOUBLERS

STOCK	FIRST SALE OF YEAR	LAST SALE OF YEAR
Arwood	8 3/4	18 7/8
Atco Chemical-Industrial Products	2 1/4	5
Banff Oil	7 3/16	15 1/2
Canaveral International	1 7/8	4
Dome Petroleum	14 1/2	33 3/8
Esquire	23 1/2	67 3/4
R. Hoe	6 7/8	30
Jefferson Construction	3 5/8	7 7/8
Monogram Industries	7 7/8	15 5/8 (almost)
Rodney Metals	8 3/4	18 5/8
Saxon Paper	7 7/8	15 5/8 (almost)
Stanrock Uranium Mines	3/4	1 3/4
Talley Industries	9 5/8	19 5/8

Only thirteen stocks of the more than one thousand listed managed to double. Of these, two reflected the big Canadian oil strike at Rainbow Lake (Banff and Dome). Esquire responded to a powerful advance in net earnings; Jefferson Construction got a merger invitation; Stanrock was sensitive to the brighter long-term outlook for uranium. Nearly every one, on inspection, will be found to have a rather small capitalization and thus be able to reflect sensitively favorable corporate developments. The main message we can get from these performers is again that it helps to start out low. *All but two* started their rise from below $10 a share!

This chapter concludes a five-year review of listed stocks that have doubled. It covers an interesting group of securities and provides the background for analysis, given in a later chapter, of the dominant and often distinguishing attributes of performance stocks. These qualities or characteristics are, in fact, seldom evident in conservative dividend-paying stocks of large, mature companies. If you seek stocks that double in a year, you often find them in the byways — not the highways!

15

1967: that wonderful, wonderful year

No year in history has better documented the thesis of *Happiness Is a Stock that Doubles in a Year* than 1967. More issues doubled or better on the New York Stock Exchange, the American Stock Exchange, and the over-the-counter market than in any earlier year. Here is the count: 163 doublers on the NYSE, 396 on AMEX, and, out of a grand total of about 50,000 issues traded or quoted at some time during the year over the counter, 800 issues doubled. What a year! And what an act to follow! The full list of outstanding performers is given in the tables at the end of this chapter.

Taking up, first, the doubling issues on the New York Stock Exchange, we must note the relatively high trading range. Of the 163 issues that doubled in calendar 1967, only 27 started out below $10 a share, whereas more than half of all the doublers on the American Stock Exchange started their 1967 rise from below $10.

Many stocks doubled in 1967 simply because speculation was rife, but our contention that doubling stocks have qualities in common is beautifully illustrated by the conglomerates. Successful speculation can be assured by following a major trend — buying the fashionable stocks as soon as their fashionable status has been defined. (And, of course, sell them, if possible, just before they go out of fashion.) Look at the list of winning conglomerates in 1967: Ametek, Fuqua Industries, Avco, Bangor Punta, City Investing, Colt Industries, General Host, Hunt Foods, Kinney National Service, Norris Industries, Penn-Dixie Cement, Philadelphia & Reading, Republic Corporation, U.S. Industries, Ward Foods, Automatic Sprinkler, Avnet, Engelhard Industries, Gulton Industries, Ling-Temco-Vought, Monogram, G. C. Murphy, Teledyne, Textron, Whittaker. Roughly one stock out of every six that doubled on the NYSE in 1967 was a conglomerate. Most justified their rights to double by recording significant gains in per share net, but there were some "dropouts" in that department, notably Litton and Automatic Sprinkler. Both of these failed to deliver the enhanced 1967 earnings forecast earlier in the year. Top conglomerate honors for performance would appear to be due to Republic Corporation, from $5\frac{1}{8}$ to $69\frac{1}{2}$; Whittaker, from $13\frac{1}{2}$ to 94; Ling-Temco, from $50\frac{1}{4}$ to 125; Ward Foods, from $13\frac{5}{8}$ to $46\frac{5}{8}$; Teledyne, from $43\frac{1}{2}$ to $139\frac{1}{4}$. It is doubtful if so many conglomerates will ever perform again so well within a twelve-month period. They had a lot going for them in 1967: (1) they were the glamour stocks of the year; (2) their earnings were increasing; (3) they got a terrific press, with new mergers and acquisitions making headlines on the financial pages almost daily; and (4) aggressive company presidents got big lineage in *Time* and *Newsweek* as well as in *Barron's, Business Week, Nation's Business,* and *Forbes.* Finally, many of the major multibranch brokerage houses added fuel to the fire by writing up conglomerates frequently and favorably in special reports and market letters. Boardroom ticker watchers saw the conglomerate symbols streak before their eyes in staccato clusters like a psychedelic trip.

Computer stocks got major billing, too, in 1967 with IBM generating big gains in earnings and market price, Control Data gaining 103 points, Scientific Data 91, American Research (corporate shepherd of Digital Equipment and Applied Dynamics) gaining 150 points, and Burroughs 97 points. Five oils deserve citation: Occidental, Belco, Coastal States Gas, Helmerich & Payne, California Liquid Gas.

The inflationary nature of our market was well illustrated by the number of realty doublers: City Investing, Madison Square Garden, Sheraton, Hilton, Hilton warrants, Holiday Inns, Hotel Corporation, Del E. Webb, General Development, and Uris Building. Among metals, also traditional beneficiaries of inflation, the list included Bunker Hill, Granby, International Mining, Pan American Sulphur, Engelhard Minerals and Benguet Consolidated.

CONSUMER STOCKS

The high general level of prosperity of 1967 was created by a full civilian economy, with a $24 billion a year war demand on top. Consumer buying power drove a whole list of NYSE shares to gains of 100 percent or more: Alberto-Culver, Arlan's Stores, Brunswick, Chock full o'Nuts, Coronet, Edison Bros., Hunt Foods, Jim Walter, Kinney

National Service, S. S. Kresge, Loew's, Mattell, Mc-
Donald's, Melville Shoe, Milton Bradley, Papercraft, Par-
ker Pen, Pueblo Supermarkets, Rayette-Faberge, Shulton,
Stokely-Van Camp, Tandy, Tootsie Roll, Unishops, Ward
Foods, King's Department Stores, and Walgreen.

Major beneficiaries of military demand included E. W.
Bliss, Colt Industries, Hazeltine Corporation, Lear Siegler,
Monarch Machine Tool, Norris Industries, Ryan Aero-
nautical, Sperry Rand, Walworth, Conrac, Chromalloy,
Ling-Temco-Vought, Monogram, Textron, Trans Interna-
tional Airlines, Warner & Swasey, and Bullard.

The above comments may serve to highlight the "hot
areas" of the 1967 NYSE market. Noticeably absent among
the stellar performers were many major industries: airlines, railroads (only Florida East Coast doubled), motor
stocks, insurance, S&L shares, building materials and
cements, gas and electric utilities, chemicals, steels,
and coppers. Even in such a great market year, the industries that contributed doubling stocks were relatively
few. Stocks that double in any year are an exclusive
breed.

1967 ON THE AMERICAN STOCK EXCHANGE

A number of market analysts have developed theories
about a relationship between the American Stock Exchange and the New York Stock Exchange. One contention is that in a bull-market year, twice as many stocks
will double on AMEX as on the NYSE. That was true in
1967: 163 on the "Big Board" and 396 on the "Curb."

Another theory is that whenever the average daily
volume of transactions (number of shares traded) on
AMEX exceeds 40 percent of that on the NYSE over a
thirty-day period, the market is headed downward. (This
occurred in March-June, 1968.) We have made no endeavor to assess the possible long-term validity of either

of these theories, but they do offer different approaches to analysis of market direction.

In any event, the quest for doublers on AMEX in 1967 was a most rewarding one. The results further document our earlier observations on the nature of stocks listed on the American Stock Exchange in Chapter 14. Because of smaller issues and smaller floating supplies of stock, frequent and sizable percentage changes in price are far more prevalent on the American Exchange than on the Big Board. The more limited supplies of stocks traded generally respond more sensitively and with more volatility to good or bad news than NYSE issues; and not infrequently, trading "pockets" can occur. There can even be evidence, on occasion, of possible manipulation in individual issues. The AMEX management, however, is quick to spot improper or unusual trading activity, aided by computer surveillance; and its disciplinary action (100 percent margin, suspension of trading, or delisting) where needed has been prompt and effective. The most spectacular 1967 performer on AMEX was Cameo-Parkway Records. This issue, quite unsupported by any evidence of significant earning power or underlying book value, rose from 2⅛ to 63⅜ (a gain of 3,000 percent) in 1967, but was suspended from trading in 1968. Justification for its high price was difficult to find, and apparently those who had sold the issue short were frantic in their endeavor to "cover." A number of other issues on AMEX advanced by 100 percent or more, some of them also without an impressive statistical causation — but Cameo broke all the records!

Stocks of merit that responded with animation to rising earnings trends included: Burns International (26¾–69), Digital Equipment (30⅜–144¼), Duval (68¼–163), Ehrenreich Photo-Optical (11½–43), Equity Funding (11¼–52¾), Famous Artists (30⅛–77⅞), R. Hoe (30–133¼), Geo. A. Hormel (28–59½), Leasco (35¼–137½), Maxson Electronics

(22½–46½), Mortgage Guaranty (23½–60⅞), Tool Research & Engineering (28¾–62½), XTRA, Inc. (50⅝–139), and Zapata Off-Shore (32¼–98¼).

If computer issues were virtuosi on the NYSE, they were a chorus on AMEX. Look at the group of 1967 doublers in this category: Computer Applications, Data-Control Systems, Digital Equipment, Leasco, Levin-Townsend Computer, Automatic Data Processing, Barry Wright, California Computer, Computer Instrument, Computer Sciences, Data Processing Financial & General, Electronic Computer Programming, G C Computer, Granite Equipment Leasing, Mohawk Data Sciences, and Randolph Computer. And most of these companies were less than five years old! Traditional and time-tested criteria for stock selection on the basis of established earnings, substantial book value, and dividend payments or expectations would have put you out in left field in any appraisal of these computer equities. A more psychedelic approach was required, and a new spectrum of price/earnings multiples!

INDUSTRIAL SPECIALISTS

If computers as a group were standouts, quite a few issues moved up 100 percent or more for reasons of their own—a new or special product, a new management, or a new approach: Cole National, keymaker to the nation; Deltona, strategic landholdings; Ehrenreich, camera importation; Equity Funding, smart merchandising of mutual funds and insurance; Federal's Inc., new management of an old department-store chain; Head Ski, the "in" sport; Inflight Motion Pictures, screens on the wing; Mary Carter Paint, gambling tables on Grand Bahama; Maxson Electronics, instant hotel bookings; Transogram, toys; Zale, leading retail credit jeweler; Career Academy, a new educational entry.

The entire list is too long to review item by item. The outstanding qualities enjoyed by the winners were popular trends, small capitalizations, and newness of product, service, technology, or management; plus a cluster of issues that just went up, riding a contagious speculation wave.

AMEX — A GOOD PLACE TO SEEK DOUBLERS

We conclude by observing that any program involving selection of stocks that can double must include intensive coverage of AMEX. This exchange appears likely to produce, for a variety of reasons set down here, twice as many doublers in any year as its more elegant brother, the NYSE. While the New York Stock Exchange represents about 80 percent of all the dollar volume of trading in listed securities in America, the American Exchange, with about 13 percent of the total dollar volume, regularly provides wider daily and annual percentage price swings in individual issues and over the entire list. The value of all stocks, common and preferred, on AMEX was $43 billion at the 1967 year end, and trading volume was 66 percent greater than in 1966.

AMEX will no doubt continue to be a happy hunting ground for speculators, as 122 new issues were admitted to listing in 1967, and the total number of issues traded there as of December 31, 1967, was 1,225.

Following are the lists of stocks that doubled in 1967 on the New York Stock Exchange and the American Stock Exchange.

NEW YORK STOCK EXCHANGE ISSUES
THAT DOUBLED (OR MORE) IN VALUE IN 1967

	1/3/67 OPEN	12/31/67 CLOSE
Adams-Millis	15 7/8	62 7/8
A. J. Industries	3 3/4	10
Alberto-Culver	18 1/2	42 1/2
Allied Products	28	57 1/4
Alside	6	13 3/8
American Bosch Arma	20 1/8	64 1/4
American Cement	8 3/8	17 3/4
American Photocopy Equipment	5 5/8	15
American Research & Development	40 3/8	191
American Ship Building	11	27 1/4
American Sterilizer	27	65 3/4
Ametek	19	53 1/2
Amphenol	19 1/2	46 3/8
Arlan's Department Stores	11 5/8	24 7/8
Atlas Corporation	2 5/8	6 1/8
Avco	22 3/4	65
Baker Oil Tools	9	18
Bangor Punta	26	52 3/4
Belco Petroleum	18	53 3/8
Benguet Consolidated	2 3/8	8 1/2
Berman Leasing	5 3/4	28 5/8
E. W. Bliss	14 7/8	29 7/8
Brunswick	7 1/4	16 7/8
Bullard	16 1/8	41 1/2
Bunker Hill	26 3/4	55 5/8
Burroughs	87 1/4	185 3/8
Chemway	6 1/2	15 3/8
Chock full o'Nuts	8 3/4	22 1/8
City Investing	46	113
Clark Oil & Refining	22 3/4	48
Coastal States Gas Producing	25 1/2	53 5/8
Colt Industries	19	62 1/4
Control Data	33 1/2	136 1/2
Coronet Industries	13 1/2	32 1/2
Cudahy	6 3/4	17
Dictaphone	25 1/2	60 3/8

	1/3/67 OPEN	12/31/67 CLOSE
Dreyfus	13 7/8	34 5/8
Duplan	6 7/8	25 3/8
Edison Bros. Stores	31 3/4	66 1/4
Fedders	13	47 3/8
Florida East Coast	7 1/8	18 1/4
Fluor	32 1/2	64 5/8
General Development	6 1/8	17 5/8
General Host (General Baking to April, 1967)	16	39 1/8
Granby Mining	29 7/8	64
Harris-Intertype	28 3/4	65 3/8
Harvey Aluminum	26 1/2	54
Hazeltine	6 5/8	21
Helmerich & Payne	9 3/4	27 1/4
Hilton Hotels	15 1/4	68
Hotel Corporation of America	3 3/4	18
Hunt Foods & Industries	20 1/8	57
Indian Head	18 5/8	41 1/4
Interco	35	72 1/8
International Mining	12 3/4	31 3/4
Jim Walter	18 3/8	54
Jostens	13	28 1/4
Keebler	23 7/8 bid	53 3/8
Kinney National Service	26 1/2	57 3/4
S. S. Kresge	38 1/4	88
Lear Siegler	20 3/4	45 1/2
Leaseway Transportation	12 1/4	25 1/2
Leesona	20 5/8	42 1/4
Lionel	2 7/8	10 1/2
Loew's Theatres	26 3/8	140 1/2
Lucky Stores	17	34 1/8
Madison Square Garden	5	11 1/4
Mattell	11 1/4	49 3/4
J. W. Mays	12	24 1/2
MCA	35 1/4	74
McDonald's	29 1/4	86 1/4
Arthur G. McKee	21 3/8	43 1/8
Melville Shoe	34 5/8	85 3/4
Mid-America Pipeline	12 3/8	28 5/8
Milton Bradley	20 3/8	58 7/8

	1/3/67 OPEN	12/31/67 CLOSE
Missouri-Kansas-Texas	5 3/4	20 1/4
Monarch Machine Tool	14 3/4	41 1/4
John Morrell	25 1/2	70 3/8
Morse Shoe	21 1/4	43 3/4
National General	12	24 5/8
Neptune Meter	26 1/2	54 1/4
Norris Industries	17 1/2	39 1/8
Occidental Petroleum	42 7/8	110 5/8
Ogden	15 1/4	42 1/8
Overnite Transportation	13 1/4	28 3/4
Pan American Sulphur	15 3/8	40 7/8
Papercraft	12	25 3/4
Parker Pen	13 1/4	28
Penn-Dixie Cement	11 3/8	29 1/8
Perfect Film & Chemical (United Whelan to June, 1967)	12 1/4	66
Philadelphia & Reading	40 3/4	92 5/8
Pueblo Supermarkets	14 1/4	31 5/8
Rayette-Faberge	31 7/8	75 7/8
Raytheon	52 7/8	105 1/4 (almost)
Reliance Elec. & Engineering	23 1/2	63 1/4
Republic Corporation	5 1/8	69 1/2
Rheem Manufacturing	24	50
Riegel Textile	18 3/8	42 3/4
Ryan Aeronautical	21 5/8	43 1/2
Seagrave	14 3/8	40 1/4
Sheller-Globe	16 3/8	34
Sheraton Corporation of America	8 7/8	29 1/2
Shulton	24 1/4	52 1/4
Sperry Rand	30	63 7/8
Standard Brands Paint	13 3/4	27 5/8
Standard Pressed Steel	23 3/4	67 3/4
Standard Prudential United	8 7/8	19 1/4
Stokley-Van Camp	19 3/4	51 3/8
Sundstrand	30	84
Symington Wayne	20 1/2	41 1/8
Tandy	14 7/8	55
Toledo Scale	19 3/8	56
Tootsie Roll Industries	13 1/2	27 5/8

	1/3/67 OPEN	12/31/67 CLOSE
Tractor Supply	10 5/8	25 1/8
TRW	45 1/2	103
Unishops	21	48 5/8
United-Carr	22 1/2	54 7/8
United Fruit	26 7/8	60
United Nuclear	18 1/4	41
United Park City Mines	2	8 3/8
U. S. Industries	14 3/4	44
Universal American	10 7/8	28 7/8
Uris Buildings	16 1/4	33 1/2
Walworth	8 1/4	17 3/4
Ward Foods	13 5/8	46 5/8
Del E. Webb	2 1/2	6 7/8

NEW YORK STOCK EXCHANGE ISSUES
SPECIAL SITUATIONS — 1967

	1/3/67 OPEN	12/31/67 CLOSE
AMK	14 3/8 AMEX trading	78
Aqua-Chem	11 AMEX trading	37
Automatic Sprinkler	25 1/2 bid OTC trading	72 3/4
Avery Products	24 7/8 bid OTC trading	50 1/8
Avnet	13 1/4 adj. 4-for-3 split	49
Baxter Laboratories	20 1/4 2-for-1 split Sept.	41
California Liquid Gas	11 bid OTC trading	23 1/4
Chromalley American	18 1/2 adj. 3-for-2 split Oct.	39 1/8
Conrac (Giannini Controls to April, 1967)	25 AMEX trading	68 7/8
Culligan	23 1/4 bid OTC trading	46 3/4

	1/3/67 OPEN	12/31/67 CLOSE
Eastern Gas & Fuel Associates	29	71 1/4
	adj. 3-for-1 split Apr.	
EG&G	24 3/4	53 7/8
	adj. 2-for-1 split Oct.	
Elastic Stop Nut	29 1/2	59 3/4
	adj. 2-for-1 split Apr.	
ELTRA	18 7/8	39 1/8
	adj. 2-for-1 split Oct.	
Engelhard Minerals & Chemical	18 3/8	49 3/8
(Engelhard Industries to	adj. 2-for-1 split Aug.	
Sept., 1967)	and 5-for-4 Jan.	
Fuqua Industries (Natco to	27 3/4	69 1/2
Feb., 1967)		
Giddings & Lewis Machine Tool	13 3/8	34
	adj. for 2-for-1 split Oct.	
A. P. Green Refractories	17 1/4	34
		(almost)
Gulton Industries	26 1/4	59 1/4
	adj. 100% stock div. July	
Handleman	16 7/8 bid	52 3/4
	AMEX trading	
Holiday Inns of America	20 1/8	53 1/4
	adj. 2-for-1 split Sept.	
King's Department Stores	12	36 7/8
	adj. 5-for-4 split June	
Ling-Temco-Vought	50 1/4	125
	adj. 3-for-2 split July	
Monogram Industries	33 3/4	71
	AMEX trading	
G. W. Murphy Industries	27 1/4	74 1/2
(Reed International to April, 1967)		
Omark Industries	11 3/4 bid	28
	OTC trading	
Ronson	14	31
	adj. 4-for-3 split June	
Sanders Associates	28 1/2	65
	adj. 2-for-1 split July	
Scientific Data Systems	45 1/2	136 1/4
	adj. 3-for-2 split June	
Simplicity Pattern	22 3/8	49
	adj. 2-for-1 split Sept.	

	1/3/67 OPEN	12/31/67 CLOSE
Teledyne	43 1/2	139 1/4
	adj. 2-for-1 split July	
Textron	25 1/4	51 7/8
	adj. 2-for-1 split Sept.	
Trans International Airlines	11 1/2 OTC	24 5/8
	adj. 2-for-1 split Sept.	
VSI	12 1/4	43
	adj. 2-for-1 split Nov.	
Walgreen	17 3/8	41 1/2
	adj. 2-for-1 split Oct.	
Warner & Swasey	22 1/8	48 1/8
	adj. 5-for-4 split July	
Whittaker	13 1/2 bid	94
	OTC trading	

AMERICAN STOCK EXCHANGE ISSUES THAT DOUBLED (OR MORE) IN VALUE IN 1967

	1/3/67 OPEN	12/31/67 CLOSE
Aberdeen Petroleum Class A	3 3/8	13 5/8
Aeronca	6 1/2	26 1/4
Aileen	6 3/4	30 3/4
Airwork	5 1/4	12 7/8
Ajax Magnethermic	18 7/8	54 3/4
All American Engineering	7 3/8	23 3/8
Allied Artists Pictures	1 3/4	10 5/8
Alloys Unlimited	19 3/4	48 7/8
Alsco Class A	6 1/2	13 5/8
Altamil	10 3/8	26
American Beverage	5 1/2 bid	11 1/4
American Petrofina Class A	9 1/4	18 1/4 (almost)
American Safety Equipment	5 1/2	14 1/8
AMREP (American Realty & Petroleum to Oct., 1967)	3 1/8 bid	12 1/2
Ansul	12 3/8	26
Anthony Pools	2 1/8	5 5/8
Apache	9 5/8	25 3/8

	1/3/67 OPEN	12/31/67 CLOSE
Apollo Industries	3 3/4	7 3/4
Applied Devices (Belock Instrument to Feb., 1967)	2 5/8	6 1/8
Arrow Electronics	2 3/4	9 3/4
Arwood	19 1/8	41 1/4
Associated Laundries of America	1 3/4	4
Associated Oil & Gas	2	6 3/4
Associated Products	10 1/2 bid	26 7/8
Atlas Corporation Warrants	1 1/2	3 7/8
Automatic Radio Manufacturing	3 bid	18 1/2
Avien	1 5/8	6 1/4
BACM Industries (British American Construction & Materials to July, 1967)	5 1/8	15 3/8
Baker Industries	25 5/8	63 7/8
Baldwin Montrose Chemical	10 1/2	23 1/8
Banner Industries	1 1/4	4
Barnwell Industries	3 7/8	10
Bartell Media	4	9 1/8
Barton's Candy	4 1/4	12 7/8
Baruch-Foster	1 5/8	6 1/2
A. S. Beck Shoe	11	25 7/8
Bell Electronics	4 3/4	32 7/8
Bergen Drug Class A	10 bid	22 7/8
Bethlehem Corporation	5 1/2	15 1/4
Birdsboro	5 5/8	15
Bloomfield Building Class A	5/8	2 3/8
Bowling Corporation of America	1 3/8	3 7/8
Bowmar Instrument	7 1/4	14 3/4
Bowser	6 bid	17 1/4
Brad Foote Gear Works	4 5/8	9 3/4
Bradford Speed Packaging & Development	16 1/2	42 5/8
Brooks & Perkins	9 3/4	34 1/4
Bunker-Ramo	8 1/8	17 1/8
William J. Burns International Detective Agency	26 3/4	69
Butler's Shoe	10 7/8	21 5/8
Buttes Gas & Oil	2 7/8	10 1/4
Cameo-Parkway Records	2 1/8	63 3/8

	1/3/67 OPEN	12/31/67 CLOSE
Castleton Industries (formerly Universal Automated Industries — exchanged share for share Oct., 1967)	1 3/8	8 1/8
CBK Industries	4 bid	10 3/8
CCI	6 1/8	26 3/8
Century Industries	5 1/8	10 1/8 (almost)
Chelsea Industries	8	27 7/8
Chief Consolidated Mining	3 1/8	7 1/4
Christiana Oil	2 3/4	5 1/2
Cinerama	3 3/8	8
Clark Cable	4 1/8	9 1/8
Clary	4 1/4	18 7/8
Clopay	5 1/2 bid	12 1/8
Coburn Corporation of America	10 3/8	32 1/8
Cohu Electronics	4 3/8	10 7/8
Cole National	14 1/2	34 3/4
Commonwealth United Class A	4 1/8	11 3/4
Community Discount Centers	5	17 3/4
Compo Industries	10	19 7/8 (almost)
CompuDyne	1 1/8	8 3/4
Computer Applications	14 3/8	42 1/2
Condec	10 7/8	41
Consolidated Leasing Corporation of America	13 1/2	39 3/4
Consolidated Oil & Gas	2 3/4	14 3/8
Consultants & Designers	11 1/8	33
Continental Connector Class A	9 1/4	28 5/8
Continental Materials	1 1/8	2 5/8
Cook Electric	7 5/8	15 3/8
Coro	9 3/8	18 3/8 (almost)
Crestmont Oil & Gas	3 3/8 bid	7 5/8
Crowley, Milner	7 3/4 bid	18 7/8
Daryl Industries	1 3/8	4 7/8
Data-Control Systems	7 3/8	18 1/8
Deltona	9 3/8	20 5/8
Detecto Scales	6 1/4	15 7/8
Dielectric Products Engineering	5 3/4	15 7/8

	1/3/67 OPEN	12/31/67 CLOSE
Digital Equipment	30 3/8	144 1/4
Diversey	12 3/8 bid	31 3/4
Dixilyn	13 1/4	32 1/8
D M H (Detroiter Mobile Homes to June, 1967)	2 3/8	5 7/8
Drug Fair-Community Drug	5 1/4	13 5/8
Duro-Test	6 3/4	15 1/2
Duval	68 1/4	163
Dynalectron	3 3/8	22 3/8
Eagle Clothes	9 7/8	20 3/4
Earl Scheib	6 7/8	13 5/8 (almost)
Edo	18 3/4	41 3/8
Ehrenreich Photo-Optical	11 1/2	43
Electronic Assistance	3 7/8	31
Electronic Research Associates Class A	4 1/8	22 7/8
Electronics Corporation of America	7	19 5/8
El-Tronics	1 3/8	5 1/4
Emery Industries	23 3/4	47 (almost)
Equity Corporation	3	6 3/8
Equity Funding Corporation of America	11 1/4 bid	52 3/4
Ero Industries	3 3/4	10
Ets-Hokin	2 3/8	6 3/4
Evans Aristocrat Industries	2 3/4	5 3/4
Exquisite Form Industries	2 5/8	6 1/4
Fairfield-Noble	7 7/8	21
Falcon Seaboard Drilling	7 1/4	18 1/4
Famous Artists Schools	30 1/8	77 7/8
Fargo Oils	2 5/8	6 15/16
Federal Resources	5 1/2	12
Federal's	4 1/4	14
Federated Purchaser	1 3/4 bid	4 3/8
Financial General	13 1/4	26 1/4 (almost)
First National Realty & Construction	3/4	1 3/4
Florida Capital	2	4 7/8
Forest City Enterprises	4 3/8	9 1/4
Fresnillo	13 1/4	36 1/2

	1/3/67 OPEN	12/31/67 CLOSE
Friendly Frost	2 5/8 bid	8 1/4
Gale Industries	1 3/4	19 5/8
Garan	6 7/8	20 1/4
GCA	29 1/8	55 1/8
General Builders	1 5/8	4 1/8
General Cinema	16 1/4	40
General Interiors	11 1/4	25 1/4
Genisco Technology	9 1/4	24 1/8
Giant Food Class A	11 3/4 bid	25 3/4
G-L Industries	9	19
Goldfield	2 3/8	8
Goodway	4 3/4	28 5/8
Gordon Jewelry Class A	16 1/4	39 3/8
Gray Manufacturing	7 1/2 bid	24 7/8
Great Lakes Chemical	3 3/4	10 3/4
Great Lakes Recreation	3 3/8	11 3/4
Greer Hydraulics	9 1/2	20 1/2
Grow Chemical	10 1/8	22 3/8
Guerdon Industries	4 5/8	13 1/8
Gulf Resources & Chemical	16 1/8	33 1/2
(Gulf Sulphur to June, 1967)		
H&B American	4 1/2	17
C. M. Hall Lamp	4 1/2	11 3/4
Harvard Industries	7 3/8 bid	49 3/8
Harvey Radio	4	23 1/4
Harvey's Stores	5 1/4	19 1/2
Head Ski	9 1/2	18 7/8
		(almost)
Heinicke Instruments	5	10 3/8
Hitco	7	45 1/4
R. Hoe	30	133 1/4
Hofmann Industries	1 3/8	5
Holly Corporation	3/4	3
George A. Hormel	28	59 1/2
House of Fabrics	3 1/4	23 5/8
Hydromatics	3 1/2	12 1/8
Hydrometals	5 5/8	33 3/8
IMC Magnetics	5 3/8	17 5/8
Industrial Plywood	3 1/8 bid	10 7/8
Inflight Motion Pictures	10 3/8	33

	1/3/67 OPEN	12/31/67 CLOSE
Inland Credit Class A	3 1/4	7 1/2
Inland Homes	2 5/8 bid	13 5/8
Interphoto Class A	14 3/8	53 1/8
Investors Royalty	4 3/8	12
Ipco Hospital Supply	11 1/2 — adj.	25 bid
	2-for-1 split December	
Iroquois Industries (International Breweries to May, 1967)	4 1/4	27 3/8
Irving Air Chute	9 3/4	20 1/8
Isram	1 3/4	7 1/4
Jackson's Minit Markets	7 bid	17 1/2
Jeannette Glass	6 3/8	14 3/8
Jefferson Lake Petrochemicals	23 1/8	59
Jetronic Industries	1 3/4	6 7/8
Kaiser Industries	9 1/8	19 1/8
D. Kaltman	3 7/8	10 1/4
Kane-Miller	3 1/2	11 5/8
Kin-Ark Oil	2 3/8	5 1/2
Kingsford	8	18
Kingston Products	4 3/8	9 1/8
Kissell Class A	3 bid	7
Kleer-Vu Industries	2 3/4	29
L'Aiglon Apparel	5 7/8 bid	29
Lafayette Radio Electronics	8 1/4	25 3/4
Lake Shore Mines	1 7/8 bid	4
La Maur	12 1/8	38
Leasco Data Processing Equipment	35 1/4	137 1/2
Lee Filter	6 1/2	14 3/4
Lee Motor Products Class A	1 3/8	5 3/4
Leece-Neville	17 3/4	36 3/8
Lenox	15 1/2	35
Lerner Stores	7	18
Levin-Townsend Computer	12 3/8	74 1/4
Lily Lynn Class A	3 1/8	7 3/4
Locke Manufacturing	5 3/4 bid	14 1/2
Lodge & Shipley	2	4 1/2
Logistics Industries (J. E. Plastics Manufacturing to Sept., 1967)	3 1/2	13 5/8
Longines-Wittnauer Watch	14 3/4 bid	66 5/8
Louis Sherry	3 1/8	7 3/8

	1/3/67 OPEN	12/31/67 CLOSE
LTV Electrosystems	13 7/8	35 1/2
Lundy Electronics & Systems	14 7/8	44 1/2
Magellan Petroleum	1 3/4	3 3/4
Mammoth Mart	11 3/4	24 1/4
Mansfield Tire & Rubber	7 7/8	20 1/2
Marlene Industries	13 3/8	45 1/8
Mary Carter Paint Class A	3 7/8	26 1/2
Class B	5 7/8	25 5/8
Maul Brothers	16 1/4	28 1/2
Maxson Electronics	22 1/2	46 1/2
McCulloch Oil	7 3/8	27
Medco Class A	7 3/8	18 1/4
MEM	14	30 1/8
Menasco Manufacturing	6 7/8	32 5/8
Merrill Island Mining	11/16	1 7/8
Microdot	18	77 3/4
Microwave Associates	22	43 5/8 (almost)
Milgo Electronic	5 3/8	14 1/8
Miller-Wohl	6 1/4	18 1/2
Milo Electronics	5 7/8	17 1/2
Missouri-Kansas-Texas Certificates	6 7/8	23 7/8
Morse Electro Products	3 3/8	11 1/2
Mortgage Guaranty Insurance	23 1/2	60 7/8
Mott's Super Markets	6 1/4 bid	12 7/8
Movie Star Class A	7 3/8 bid	15 1/4
MPO Videotronics Class A	6	15
National Bowl-O-Mat	1 bid	3
National Company	6 1/4 bid	15 1/2
National Equipment Rental	4 1/2	104 1/2
National Presto Industries	16 1/4	55 7/8
Needham Packing	4 3/4	13 5/8
New Park Mining Co.	4 5/8	11 5/8
Newark Electronics Class A	7 1/4	14 3/4
NMS Industries (Ross Products to Sept., 1967)	1 7/8	19 3/8
North Canadian Oils	2 3/4	5 3/8 (almost)
Nuclear Corporation of America	2	5 5/8
Nytronics	14 1/8	42 1/2

	1/3/67 OPEN	12/31/67 CLOSE
OKC (Oklahoma Cement Co. to Jan., 1967)	10 7/8	21
Originala	6 3/4	39 3/4
O'Sullivan Rubber	8 3/4 bid	27 7/8
Oxford Finance	4 1/2	20 3/4
Pacific Industries	2 1/4	5 1/8
Packer's Super Markets	6 1/8	12 1/8 (almost)
Pancoastal Petroleum	13/16	2 3/4
Park Electrochemical Class A	3 3/4	8 1/8
Pato Consolidated Gold Dredging	3 3/16	10 3/8
Pentron Electronics	1 1/2	3 1/4
Philips Industries	7 1/8	31 3/8
Phillips Screw	6 1/2 bid	25 3/8
Phoenix Steel	12 1/4	28 1/2
Pioneer Aerodynamic Systems	10 3/8	23 3/8
Pioneer Plastics	5 1/2	14 7/8
Plant Industries	2 7/8 bid	6 3/8
Pneumatic Scale	11 1/2 bid	25 1/4
Polarad Electronics	3 3/4	11 3/4
Poloron Products Class A	10 3/4	37 3/8
Potter Instrument	13 7/8	31 3/4
Ramer Industries	2 3/8	5 3/8
Rapid-American	8 3/4	21
Redman Industries	4 1/4	15 1/4
Reeves Industries	2 1/4	7 1/8
Remco Industries	2 5/8 bid	8 1/8
Resistoflex	12	23 7/8 (almost)
Restaurant & Waldorf Associates	4 7/8	27 3/4
Retail Center of The Americas	4 bid	10 3/4
RIC Group	1 1/8	3
Roblin Steel Class A	4 3/8	9 1/8
Rodney Metals	18 1/2	39 1/4
Royal American Industries	1 1/4	2 1/2
Royal Industries	14 1/8	43 1/4
Royal School Laboratories	4 1/2	9 3/4
Rudy Manufacturing	18 7/8 bid	66 1/4
Rusco Industries	2 1/8	11 1/2
Russeks	1 1/2	3 3/8

	1/3/67 OPEN	12/31/67 CLOSE
Ryan Consolidated	5 7/8	14 7/8
Ryerson & Haynes	5	10 3/8
Salem-Brosius	2 5/8	8 1/8
Saxon Paper	15 7/8	34
Sayre & Fisher	4	8 1/8
Scope Industries	7 1/4	15 1/4
Season-all Industries	1 7/8	10
Seeman Brothers	4 1/8	9 7/8
Siboney	3/8	3
Sigma Instruments	14 3/8	32 5/8
Silvray-Litecraft	1 5/8	12 7/8
Simkins Industries	4 1/2	10 7/8
Skyline	13 1/2	56
Southern Gulf Utilities	10 1/2	24
Southern Realty & Utilities	1 3/4	5 1/2
Spector Industries	9 1/2	18 5/8 (almost)
Standard Dredging	5 3/8	12 3/4
Standard International	10 7/8	23 7/8
Standard Products	18 1/2	37 1/4
Standard-Thomson	5 3/8 bid	15
Stanrock Uranium Mines	1 3/4	4
Stelma	9 1/4	37 3/4
Stephan	2 1/2 bid	9 1/8
Sterling Precision	1 7/8	7 5/8
Sternco Industries Class A	12 3/4	40 3/4
Struthers Wells	12	26 1/8
Stylon	4 5/8	18 1/2
Sunair Electronics	4 1/2	11 1/2
Supercrete	1/2	2 1/16
Superscope	9 3/4	31 3/8
Supronics	2	9 1/8
Swanee Paper	4 7/8 bid	10 3/4
Systron-Donner	17 1/2	42 7/8
Talley Industries	19 3/4	59 1/2
Technicolor	8 1/4	26 1/4
TelePrompter	13 1/4	34 3/4
Tenney Engineering	2 1/4	7 7/8

	1/3/67 OPEN	12/31/67 CLOSE
Texstar	2 7/8	16 1/2
Thompson-Starrett	2 5/8	6 3/4
Tool Research & Engineering	28 3/4	62 1/2
Trans-Beacon	2	5 3/8
Transcontinental Investing	1 3/4	18
Transogram	4 1/4	23
United Aircraft Products	9 3/4	28 3/8
United Asbestos	2 5/16	7 3/8
United Foods	4 3/4 bid	15 5/8
United Improvement & Investing	2 7/8	11 3/4
United Piece Dye Works	2 7/8	9 1/2
U. S. Filter	5	16 3/8
U. S. Leasing	4	14 5/8
U. S. Polymeric	10 1/2	24 5/8
U. S. Rubber Reclaiming	3 1/4	13 3/8
Universal Container Class A	4 3/4	12 3/8
Vernitron	8	55
Victoreen	6 1/2	14 3/8
Viewlex Class A	6 1/8	18
Volume Merchandise	8 3/8	17
VTR	1 5/8	5 3/4
Waitt & Bond	5/8	2 3/4
Waltham Precision Instruments	2 1/4	14 3/4
Wentworth Manufacturing	2 1/2 bid	5
Westbury Fashions	2 3/4 bid	7 3/8
Western Nuclear	16 3/8	32 7/8
Wheelabrator	16 7/8	38 1/4
White Eagle International	1 1/4	2 7/8
Wieboldt Stores	12 5/8	26 5/8
Wood Industries	10	27 5/8
Woods Corporation	12 3/8	36
World Color Press	13 1/4	29 7/8
Wright-Hargreaves Mines	7/8	1 3/4
XTRA	50 5/8	139
Zale	21 3/4	44 5/8
Zapata Off-Shore	32 1/4	98 1/4
Zero Manufacturing	10 1/4	25 3/8
Zion Foods	1 7/8	4 1/8

AMERICAN STOCK EXCHANGE ISSUES
SPECIAL SITUATIONS — 1967

	1/3/67 OPEN	12/31/67 CLOSE
Allen Electric & Equipment	17 1/2 listed only on Midwest SE	62 3/8
Automatic Data Processing	25 bid OTC trading	64 3/8
Bali	10 3/4 OTC trading	28 1/2
Barry Wright	8 3/8 adj. 2-for-1 split	28 1/2
Big Apple Supermarkets	7 3/8 bid OTC trading	21
California Computer Products (25% stock div. April, 1967, split 2 for 1 Nov., 1967)	12 1/4 adj.	44 7/8
Career Academy	13 1/2 bid (OTC) adj. 100% stock div. Oct.	51 7/8
Carol Wire & Cable (25% stock div. Feb. 1967)	12 adj.	58
Computer Instrument	9 bid OTC trading	37 1/4
Computer Sciences	11 3/16 adj. 2-for-1 split May	62 1/4
Cosmodyne (50% stock div. paid Dec., 1967)	11 3/8 adj.	25 1/2
Data Processing Financial & General	23 1/2 bid OTC trading	129 1/2
DeJur-Amsco Class A	6 7/8 bid OTC trading	16 5/8
Del Laboratories	6 7/8 bid OTC trading	15 1/4
Denny's Restaurant (25% stock div. Jan., 1967, split 2 for 1 Nov., 1967	11 1/2 adj.	46 3/4
Eckerd Drugs	15 1/2 bid adj. 100% stock div. June	49 on AMEX all year

	1/3/67 OPEN	12/31/67 CLOSE
Elcor Chemical	10 3/4 bid OTC trading	53 1/4
Electronic Computer Programming	24 1/2 bid OTC trading	51 3/8
Fisher Governor	28 OTC trading	57 1/2
Gaylords National Corp.	7 1/8 OTC trading	20 1/2
G C Computer	9 1/2 OTC trading	35 5/8
Gilbert Systems	5 3/4 OTC trading	14 1/2
Glasrock Products	7 1/4 OTC trading	35 3/8
Granite Equipment Leasing	9 3/4	53 1/2
Huyck	17 3/4 OTC trading	54 3/8
La Pointe Industries	4 7/8 OTC trading	18
Marshall Industries	4 1/2 OTC trading	44 7/8
Mesa Petroleum	14 1/2	42 3/4
Mohawk Data Sciences	31 1/2	170
P & F Industries	5 3/8 bid OTC trading	15 5/8
Penn Engineering & Manufacturing	10 1/2 bid OTC trading	23 1/4
Planning Research	10 adj. 2-for-1 split Oct.	43
Ramada Inns	8 3/4 bid OTC trading	27 3/8
Randolph Computer	16 bid OTC trading	53 7/8
Reda Pump	11 bid adj. 2-for-1 split Nov.	31 1/4
R F. Communications	18 3/4 bid OTC trading	38 3/4
Richford Industries	6 7/8 bid OTC trading	20
Sav-A-Stop	13 3/4 bid OTC trading	26 3/4

	1/3/67 OPEN	12/31/67 CLOSE
Scurry-Rainbow Oil	19	48 1/2 on AMEX all year
Skaggs Drug Centers	11 1/4 bid OTC trading	29
Susquehanna	6 3/4 bid OTC trading	65 1/8
Telex	5 1/4 bid OTC trading	15 7/8
Tyco Laboratories	22 3/4 bid OTC trading	105 1/2
Union Corporation	6 1/4 bid OTC trading	17 1/2
Varo	12 1/2 bid OTC trading	40
Visual Electronics	8 1/4 bid OTC trading	24 3/4
Vocaline Company of America	4 bid OTC trading	17
Wackenhut	7 1/8 bid OTC trading	28 5/8
Welded Tube of America	4 1/2 bid OTC trading	9 1/4
Whitehall Electronics	3 bid OTC trading	14
Wyandotte Industries	12 Traded on NYSE Jan. 1 to Aug. 22; then trans- ferred to AMEX	21 1/4
Wyle Laboratories	8 bid OTC trading	29 3/4

16

characteristics and habitats of stocks that can double in a year

This book, as you must know by now, is based upon the novel yet logical premise that stocks that double in 1962, 1967, or any other year have certain qualities or characteristics in common. They do not fall into any standard pattern of shares, making up the Dow-Jones Industrial Average or the general list of marketable equities. They will notably outperform in a representative year utility, rail, telephone, cement, or steel company shares; and they will handsomely reward those who recognize potential doublers early, buy boldly, and sell at the right time.

As a preliminary exercise, we suggest that you review swiftly the lists of stocks that doubled in the years 1962-

67, paying particular attention to 1967. This was the year in which more stocks doubled on the NYSE, AMEX, and over the counter than in any other year in history. These exciting winners, hundreds of them last year, have a real message for speculators because they have led to refinements in our system of selection. We now have many more attributes, characteristics, and bench marks for the selection of stocks that may double than we had when this book first saw the light of its publication day, on July 31, 1967. Our theory is now better documented, and we are more confident of our ability to single out hopeful market leaders in the months and years ahead.

One of the refinements in our theory is an all-inclusive one. Though we recognize that the guts of security evaluation is found in projection of the direction, the extent, and the persistency of corporate earnings, we are increasingly impressed with the power and impact of emotional and psychological forces affecting the market. For example, as this particular chapter was written, trading on the New York Stock Exchange recorded an all-time daily high of 20,410,000 shares; and stocks rose in a 10-day period more than 50 points on the DJIA. In early April, the market had corrected, and offset, a market downspin evident during the entire first quarter of 1968. How could this happen? Why did it occur? Did corporate earnings evidence a notable uptrend? No! Was money any cheaper? No! Were taxes about to be reduced? No—they were increased by a 10 percent surtax. All this market euphoria, in fact, stemmed from emotional hope—hope that there would be peace. Hope that Ho Chi Minh meant what he said when he agreed to enter negotiation about a complete bombing cease. This was merely a harbinger of peace. No one believed that Ho would be a "patsy" at the bargaining table or that the war would end summarily. But the hopes of America that our military casualties would end, that our expenditures for war effort in Vietnam would cease — these hopes, psychological and emotional in character, sent our market zooming and caused millions of speculators to ignore the basic economic facts that: (1) corporate earnings might be lower in 1968, (2) taxes would rise, (3) strikes and the cost of labor would increase by 6 percent, (4) the rediscount rate had been raised to 5 percent (always heretofore a bear signal), (5) interest rates were the highest in forty years, inhibiting corporate expansion and commercial and residential building construction, (6) the bowing out of President Johnson from the 1968 Presidential race left great uncertainty about the fiscal, monetary, economic, political, and military direction of our government, under a new President in January, 1969, (7) racial tensions and high unemployment among the Negro and Puerto Rican population clouded the overall vigor and stability of our economy, and (8) railroad earnings, down in 1967, showed no basis for major improvement in 1968.

The above contrast between the psychological and logical elements affecting our economy in spring, 1968, were marshalled to establish one point: the mood of the market is far more important, at any critical time, than statistical data. So don't fight a jumpy market with facts. Following emotional trends in the short run is far more conducive to capital gains than incisive evaluation of balance sheets and earnings statements. Therefore, before you start deciding on an individual stock, consider the emotional and — derivative of that — the fashionable or popular forces holding market sway. The shooting of a President, the certainty of peace or war, the concern over race riots, the distrust of the U.S. dollar, all are emotional factors.

I cite the importance of emotionally induced popularity and fashion because I erred in that department in the 1967 edition of this book. I thought that both life stocks and savings-and-loan shares would surge in 1967 for statistical reasons; but they didn't because they were emotionally hung up. They were no more in fashion than hoop skirts or celluloid collars! Computers, oils, electronics, food, and scientific stocks were in the swim last year; so major market entry, to be speculatively successful, should have been in those fields.

Having stressed the importance of speculation in emotionally hot market areas, we now move to more mathematical and long-range factors. Even in favored market sectors, the shares that move most energetically will possess some or most of the following characteristics which we have gleaned by close observation of stellar performers in bygone years:

1. Merger-minded large companies in a bull-market year will advance far more than shares in conservative or traditional lines. Occidental Petroleum is more likely to zoom than Standard of New Jersey; Ward Foods than General Foods; City Investing than Scott Paper; National Industries than Long Island Lighting; Greater Washington Investment than Westinghouse Electric. The goal of a conglomerate is to achieve an above-average P/E multiple; when it does, it rewards early speculators in an above-average way.

2. Prefer low-priced stocks. The odds favoring a stock doubling from $5 to $10 are two to one over a stock at $50 moving to $100. If you review the big gainers in every bull-market year, you'll find that most of them started below $5 on AMEX and below $10 on the NYSE (and below $4 OTC).

3. Prefer and seek aggressive young imaginative managements willing to innovate in research, products, markets, and methods. The most aggressive managements are usually found in younger, earlier-stage companies, where ambitious and talented men have left bigger companies to start their own. Look at the young computer outfits that under leadership of gifted émigrés from IBM,

Honeywell, or Sperry Rand have become fabulously successful; the graduates of Litton that have become conglomerate virtuosi!

4. Stick to companies in which management owns 30 percent or more of the stock. In such cases, the big drive is to make the stock worth more, not to pass out high-bracket salaries and comfortable pensions to oldsters en route to retirement. Management should be hungry, not sleek and satisfied.

5. Seek companies with small capitalizations. If you watch the market action of Chicago & Northwestern, Greatamerica, Financial Federation, H. C. Bohack, Cameo-Parkway, Solitron, Burroughs, Deltona, and especially the younger, newer companies, OTC, you will note that as earnings gain, and good news is circulated, these companies, with relatively few shares outstanding, will respond far more rapidly to aggressive buying than companies with huge capitalizations, such as General Motors, with 286 million shares traded. Both leverage and scarcity provide superior potentials for built-in gain in small capitalized companies, especially if their earnings are in a strong uptrend.

6. Even when large capitalizations are outstanding, market gains can be accelerated if most of the stock is closely held and floating supply limited. This situation might apply to such companies as Polaroid, Valley Metallurgical, Alloys Unlimited, Superior Oil, Syntex, Poloron, Mine Safety Appliances, etc.

7. Breakthroughs are dynamic whether they are scientific, technological, commercial, or mineralogical. A new oil strike can make a stock like Banff Oil, Consolidated Oil & Gas, Canadian Homestead, or Occidental. Texas Gulf gained 100 points on a mineral strike at Timmins; Poloroid grew great on patents; so did Photon, National Patents Development, Brun Sensor, Kentucky Fried Chicken, Velcro, Recognition Equipment, Xerox, Wang

Laboratories, Dymo Industries, Valley Metallurgical, Tool Research & Engineering, etc. Keep looking for companies that have staked out a significant new material or mineral or scientific advance.

8. Sponsorship is important. You may not learn at the outset about a progressive young industrial company but when it gets written up in the statistical reports of major brokerage and investment houses, and is first purchased by mutual funds, you'll observe market recognition, strength, and sponsorship. Appearance of this sponsorship may be an excellent time to make a purchase with considerable assurance of success.

9. The market always prefers the new to the old. Consequently, as between buying the shares of an old company in a possible turnaround position, or shares in a newer, lesser known, but dynamic enterprise, prefer the newcomer! Its merits may be less documented, but its market acceptance may be far more aggressive and rewarding.

10. Other things being equal, prefer growth companies. These should double their sales in five years and advance their net earnings by 15 percent or more annually compounded. And they are usually found in industries themselves growing at least twice as fast as the Gross National Product.

11. Excellent gains can often be achieved by buying OTC stocks some months in advance of their application for exchange listing.

12. Prefer the newer industries. Today, these would include offshore drilling, oceanography, extended-care hospitals, leasing companies, laser-optics, instrumentation, exotic metals, maintenance and service companies.

13. Watch for turnaround industries — those in a doldrum for two or three years, thoroughly downtrodden and neglected, but with capability for a dramatic about-face. In 1968-69, cement shares, life stocks, certain S&L shares

and land companies might qualify, if earnings display genuine uptrends.

14. Special situations, including takeovers, which we've already discussed intensively, are rich fields for potential doublers.

15. Be alert for new issues, especially if they relate to scientific or marketing advances, or are industries in which public offerings are a novelty.

Here then is a rough catalog of some of the qualities you will usually find in stocks that have doubled or may do so. The great majority of all securities display few of these characteristics. That's why they will display price variations in a year of only 25 to 35 percent. The above list not only contains valuable bench marks but indicates as well the general areas in which you should be conducting a continuous search for possible doublers. We have prepared an interesting random list of shares selected for possible upside velocity. You will find this in Chapter 18.

17
life-insurance stocks

We're now approaching the most exciting part of this book—the listing of forty-five stocks that, in light of past performance of stocks with similar characteristics, might possibly perform above average or even double in 1968-69.

A major problem exists, however, in the production of any hard-cover book. After the manuscript has been completely prepared, edited, and approved by the publisher, it still takes 120 days to print, bind, and jacket the book for delivery to mailroom or bookstore. In this time, a list of stocks can display some wide price variations. There also are those readers who may say (if the stocks go up) that we waited till the last minute to insert the list so we would be certain to select sure winners. If only we *could* do that! That is definitely not the case. Every stock given honorable mention in the next chapter was researched for some time, and picked out from many others, in the same general price range, industry, or phase in corporate development.

The actual prices given are as of the close of the market on May 31, 1968. It therefore follows that our expectation is that a goodly number of these issues will perform well, and possibly double by or before June 1, 1969. Those that do gain 100 percent or more in this twelve-month interval will, of course, qualify for *Happiness Is a Stock that Doubles in a Year.* The primary basis for presenting any list at all is that we believe that, in the twelve months under discussion, the market will be confidently bullish after a possible mid-year lull in 1968. It is our theory that sometime in this interval the Dow-Jones Industrial Average will cross 1,150; and that several industries will perform outstandingly: oil, certain minerals, computers, realty, building materials, science and instrumentation, pre-prepared foods, leisure pursuits, homes and hospitals for the aged, certain conglomerates, and life insurance.

We did in fact go down the line for life-insurance stocks in our 1967 edition. With admirable logic, we stated that life insurance was an outstanding growth industry, gaining 7 percent or so in adjusted net income year after year. Further, in January, 1967, life stocks were selling, despite a fine series of annual gains in earnings and assets, at 35 percent below their 1964 highs. This seemed all wrong so we predicted notable gains in this market sector. We selected some stocks that fitted our formula of superior growth, energetic management, heavy stock ownership by management, compact capitalizations, etc. And what happened? Nothing! Actually, the shares sold off a bit and were a complete drag on the other stocks in the list, most of which advanced briskly. Which brings us to 1968-69. If life-insurance stocks didn't move in 1967, are they poised to mend their ways now, and to catch up on all the gaining they should have done a year ago? Our answer is yes! The fundamental factors in their favor are more impressive than ever. Why should we go out on a limb two years in a row on a cluster of life-stock standard issues? Here are some of the reasons:

STATURE AND COVERAGE

Life insurance remains among the fastest-growing major industries in America, its profit picture moving forward at a rate more than twice that of GNP. It now boasts over $190 billion in assets, with more than a trillion dollars of life insurance in force. Life insurance is one of the three major building blocks in any sound family thrift program (the others are savings account and equity investment). Under our standard of living, and to provide proper family protection in a climate of continuous inflation, the need for life protection is constantly rising. Yet, even today, most American families are underinsured, with average life coverage as of the end of 1967, of $17,100. Adequate minimum coverage in the opinion of family-planning experts should be three to four times the annual gross earnings of the breadwinner.

Not only is there the expectation of steadily increasing sales of life insurance, but many of the most progressive companies in the business are expanding their claim on the savings dollars of Americans by offering mutual funds or variable annuities in a package with life insurance. Thus sales volumes are increasing and lapses reduced because the buyer has dedicated himself to a complete financial program with rewarding long-term goals, a program he is reluctant to give up.

EARNING POWER

The earnings of life companies come from three sources:
(1) investment income and capital gains, (2) tight control of operating costs, and (3) improvement in mortality
experience. We'll take these up one at a time.

A life company gets investment income from interest,
dividends, plus gains from its investment portfolio. The
portfolio, in turn, consists of legal reserve funds held
virtually in trust for account of policyholders; those sums
making up the company's capital and surplus funds; and
annual additions to those funds created by accretions of
undistributed gains from operations each year.

To clarify this, suppose that Sunny Life Insurance Company has $80 million in legal reserves, $10 million in capital and surplus, and added $500,000 to capital funds from
1967 operations. The company is, we shall assume, obli-
gated to guarantee a return of 3½ percent on all reserve
funds, but legally privileged to retain all investment earnings above that rate. Here's roughly how the investment
earnings for the company would be generated in 1968:

		ESTIMATED RATE OF INVESTMENT RETURN	INCOME TOTAL
RESERVES	$80,000,000	5%	$4,000,000
	(Less 3½% assured to policyholders)		2,800,000
	Net to Company		$1,200,000
CAPITAL & SURPLUS	$10,500,000		525,000
(Net to Company in full)			
Total investment income to Company (before taxes)			$1,725,000

All of this $1,725,000 accrues to the stockholders of
Sunny Life. If it had a million shares outstanding, per
share pretax net would be $1.72. The 5 percent rate is

quite realistic as many companies earned that and more on investments in 1967; and the average rate for the entire industry in that year was 4.85 percent. As this is written in 1968, bond interest rates are at a forty-year high so that most companies are making new investments to yield about 6½ percent. Consequently life companies will be generating investment income on new funds at the highest rates in forty years, producing predictably higher annual earnings. Note, too, the leverage here: each $1 in capital funds benefits from the overage in investment earnings (above 3½ percent) of $8 in reserve funds.

While many industries are in a cost squeeze, life companies, utilizing automated and computerized equipment, have consistently been able to hold their costs down to approximately 17 percent of gross income. This is a most attractive ratio. The industry has been notably free of labor problems, so that union difficulties and work stoppages have been rare. The majority of life-company employees are women, and wages, hours, fringe benefits, and working conditions in the industry have been excellent. The most important single operating cost is sales commissions, averaging around 43 percent of gross income; and the total amount of this item varies in almost direct ratio with new business placed in the books.

Life-insurance policies have mortality rates built into them. Each policy is based on the statistical knowledge that a certain number of people per 1,000, in any group, will die in any year. This mathematical expectation is called a mortality rate. If, however, policyholders live longer than their estimated life spans (on which premium rates are in part calculated) then the issuing company makes a profit from two sources: (1) the policyholder will continue to pay premiums for more years than expected, and (2) these additional premiums and their investment, plus continued interest earnings on the policyholder's reserves, which are kept intact until death or other policy settlement occurs, enhance earnings and contribute additions to surplus of the issuing company.

For most of this century, mortality rates were improving; people were living longer and many diseases such as typhoid, tuberculosis, and poliomyelitis were conquered. This improvement has flattened out, since 1960, because of continuing high-rate fatalities due to heart disease and cancer. If and when breakthroughs in prevention and cure of these major killers occurs, then mortality rates may show significant improvements.

Other factors favoring life-company-share investment are: (1) A depression-proof business — people place a high priority on their payment of life premiums; (2) no annual models, no product or plant depreciation or obsolescence; (3) each sale brings the company income for years to come; (4) remarkable diversification both in investment portfolios and in the fact that premium income is derived from people of all ages, professions, or vocations, and usually living in broad geographical areas; (5) diligent state regulation, assuring solvency of companies; (6) well-managed investment portfolios in the finest fixed income and, increasingly, equity securities; (7) life insurance is selling to the huge youth market — young people who should live long, and pay premiums for many years.

For these reasons and because, for the twenty years prior to 1964, life stocks far outperformed the Dow-Jones Average in percentage of gain, we are solidly in favor of life-insurance stocks, and we believe that between May 31, 1968, and June 1, 1969, our selections, outlined more fully in Chapter 18, may well double.

18

45 candidates
for doubling
in 1968-69

This is the chapter you've been waiting for, of course. All of the nicely reasoned material presented earlier on conglomerates, computers, convertibles, puts, and calls is really just a long prelude to our main task—the application of these criteria to the selection of stocks with above-average capability for doubling in 1968-69.

Before we narrow our choices down to certain industries and individual issues, we'd like to make a few pertinent general observations. First, there is a long-term upward bias in the stock market which has resulted in the steady increase in value of a representative list of seasoned stocks at the rate of roughly 9 percent annually (including dividend reinvestment but excluding taxes) compounded since 1920. To fuel this uptrend, several new logs have been added to the fire. We now have:

1. A built-in inflation in our economy, raising prices about 4 percent annually.

2. Steadily rising per-capita income, so that thousands of newcomers with savings are entering the market each year.

3. An upsurging institutional demand for stocks — with $45 billion now in mutual funds, much more than that in endowment and pension funds, not to mention trust and estate funds.

4. Twenty-five million individual stockholders.

5. A rising percentage of investment in stocks by endowed institutions (the average university endowment fund today is composed of over 55 percent in common stocks, against less than 30 percent in 1940 — and the endowment funds themselves are vastly larger).

6. A pattern of corporation finance in which roughly four dollars in new corporate debt securities are issued each year for each new dollar of common stock sold or underwritten.

7. A pattern in taxation for high-bracketeers that makes gains from market speculation (taxable at 25 percent tops) preferable to income from salary, commissions, or dividends.

What we are really describing in the aggregate is a condition whereby demand for stocks is outrunning supply, inducing a quite predictable across-the-board rise in stock prices on the grounds of scarcity alone.

Another powerful factor in the stock market today is the relative youth of our investors and speculators and, even more influential, the young age of many leading analysts and partners in brokerage and investment banking houses, as well as members of management of the big funds. These youngsters are eager for the new and are bold risk-takers. They have only heard about the Great Depression, which is vastly different from experiencing it. They're accustomed to seeing stocks go up; and in their generation, the big swings have been in new industries — electronics, photocopy, computers, convenience foods, motels, service industries, publishing, and the like. The younger set is prone to place far greater accent on potential future earnings, and on new glamorous and unseasoned issues, than on such old-fashioned criteria as book values, working capital, or dividend yields. Further, there is a much more diversified shopping list for speculators today than even a decade ago — shares in dozens of new industries that have gone public, myriads of convertible bonds and preferreds, several hundred warrants to choose from, plus 30 million share put-and-call contracts a year.

Speculation has also become high fashion, and at a cocktail, dinner, or poolside party the favorite topic of conversation, after the weather and gossip, is no longer politics, foreign affairs, art, or literature but "the market." If you can't talk sagely about Control Data, nuclear explosions for oil, Occidental Petroleum, Kentucky Fried Chicken, University Computing, African gold stocks or Gerald Tsai, you're just not with it! And how can you cope with those boasters who recite their market "killings," mythical or real, unless you too have a few "performance" equities going for you?

On a dozen counts, the market can be (1) a promising arena for the gleaning of speculative profits; (2) a fashionable diversion; (3) a zestful antidote for boredom; and (4) with a little luck, quite rewarding if you buy the right stocks in the right year.

Assuming that you are a speculator — you shouldn't be reading this book if you're not, that you prefer to be an informed one; that you agree never to buy on a casual tip; that you aim to have a good reason based on adequate research for every buy or sell decision you make; that you have funds for speculation you can afford to lose in their entirety; and that you won't moan eternally about losses you are bound to incur from time to time — then, and only then, are you ready to risk your dough on stocks that may double in a year but that can also go down, down, down.

Though this book presents a lot of ideas about speculation and some theories useful in achieving superior market results, speculation is still more art than science. Luck plays a large part in speculation. If anybody really *knew* about investments, there would never be any such thing as a margin call and all stocks that informed people purchased would do nothing but go up! Don't expect the moon, and when you incur losses, remember you'll have plenty of company! The market can be a slide as well as an escalator.

It is now stock-picking time for your author and mentor. We're nervy enough to have assembled a list of forty-five stocks that, hopefully, have a better chance to double between now and June 1, 1969, than most of the 35,000 other issues traded on exchanges or over the counter in the United States and Canada. What an assignment! The "Impossible Dream" if there ever was one! Undaunted, however, and emboldened by the great success of the original edition of *Happiness Is a Stock that Doubles in a Year*, we do humbly submit our nominations for doubling in the twelve-month period from the date of their selection for this book.

FAVORED INDUSTRIES

As noted earlier, each year brings forth a few standout industries, and individual stocks within these have performed spectacularly. What are the more probable leading industries in 1968-69 — the ones that, beginning June 1, 1968 (when all the manuscript material was completed, edited, and sent to galleys), might soar within twelve months?

Our view is that the fashionable industry leaders in 1968-69 may be oils, computers and software, electronics, life insurance, medical care and cure, natural resources, science and instrumentation, oceanography, aircraft supplies, and, perhaps, building materials.

OIL COMPANIES

We think oil will continue in strong demand, that oil prices will advance, and that oil is a good inflation trend. We have winnowed seven hopeful candidates: Occidental Petroleum, White Shield, Clinton Oil, Canadian Homestead Oils (a repeat from the first edition), Consolidated Oil & Gas, Hudson's Bay Oil & Gas, and Canadian Superior Oil, another repeat.

Occidental Petroleum. We are still a little crestfallen that we omitted Occidental Petroleum from the book last year. Believe it or not, we weighed including either Bausch & Lomb or Occidental. We selected Bausch & Lomb, only to watch it sputter while Occidental rocketed! There seems to be a mystical driving force behind OXY which greatly resembles Dr. Armand Hammer. A controversial figure, with a skilled and diversely talented team of deputies, he seems to be able to play money, mergers, and corporate management by ear. Now third in sulphur, important in fertilizer, significant in petrochemicals, with huge new divisions—Island Creek Coal and Hooker Chemical, acquired in 1967-68 — and one of the richest oil stakeouts in Libya, with flowing gushers, vast reserves, and pipelines to the sea, OXY might double once again in 1968-69 if only on its virtuosity, momentum, and rising earnings. At 47¾ on May 31, 1968, OXY starts out at a little too high a price for easy doubling, but it sure is a difficult stock for avid speculators to neglect. Investigate OXY in any event. It is listed on the NYSE.

Canadian Homestead Oils. This low-price issue, listed on AMEX, does not appear to have gone as far as it will. The CHO has a good stake in sulphur at Panther River, Alberta, from a gas whose hydrogen content is exceedingly high; it has extensive coal interests in Western Alberta; it owns 161,280 acres on Cape Breton Island on which oil may be found; it has 489,000 acres in offshore Newfoundland, wildcatable; it has 1.6 million Arctic acres; it has significant acreage at Rainbow and Zama Lakes. As a natural-resource long shot, CHO deserves a more detailed inspection. It doubled in 1967, and should attract an increasing market following. A low-priced speculation with many facets for gain.

Consolidated Oil & Gas is a relatively small oil and gas producer with real estate as a secondary string to its bow. On November 30, 1967, it was reported to have oil reserves of 8.46 million barrels — a sizable gain over the 3.58 million reported a year earlier. It also has significant gas reserves (about 160 billion CF November 30, 1967). In the Bell Creek field in southern Montana, CGS has been quite successful. Its Eagle County Development Corporation is a developer and marketer of land; and its 100 percent owned subsidiary is searching for uranium in some 30,000 net claim acres in four western states. Earnings are improving and the stock has attracted a lively following on AMEX — about 4.6 million shares outstanding.

OIL DRILLING COMPANIES

There are a number of oil companies that have gained considerable stature in the past five years by using, in a substantial way, drilling money supplied by wealthy individuals. By joining in partnership with an oil-production company, a person in a 50 percent and higher tax bracket can achieve a tax saving in the first year of $7,000 or more on each $10,000 invested in a drilling program. This tax benefit is made possible by permissible deduction of intangible items incurred in drilling for oil in a given year, whether or not oil is produced. The end result is that the oil company that arranges and manages the program gets around a 50 percent interest in the total oil produced, if any, by putting up only 15 to 20 percent of the drilling money.

The general practice of oil companies is to drill most of their wells as offsets to existing producing wells. In this way, a rather high percentage of wells drilled may be expected to become "commercial," and to bring tax-sheltered income (after 27½ percent depletion tax) to company and individuals.

Companies that have gathered large sums of drilling money from individual partners include McCulloch Oil, Apache, Prudential, Clinton, White Shield, King Resources, among others. All of these have done quite well, but on the basis of their drilling results, expansion of production, and the lower current market range of their shares, it might appear that two of these, *Clinton Oil* and *White Shield* commons, are more logical candidates for doubling in 1968-69, and they are included in our screened list. White Shield, in addition to oil, has some real estate, and a drilling equipment company. Both Clinton and White Shield are traded OTC.

In Canada there are two oil stocks that have great spreads of land, and major representation in oil production in most of the proved oil regions of the Dominion. It would take pages to describe the huge land play of each; but you can get the details from most recent annual reports or from one of the statistical services.

Canadian Superior Oil was included in the 1967 edition of *Happiness*. It didn't double, but it still has the potential for 1968-69. Canadian Superior trades both in Toronto and on AMEX. Many regard it as the best oil stock in Canada.

The second stock, *Hudson's Bay Oil & Gas*, is an offshoot of the oldest company in North America, Hudson's Bay Company, which began business in 1670. In almost every sector of Canada this company has either oil production or broad swaths of oil-prone land. The shares trade in the Montreal Exchange and are subject to Equalization Tax, if bought by American citizens. If the issue traded regularly in New York, it would command a far higher price, and it is probably less likely to go down than almost any other stock we've nominated.

COMPUTER-ORIENTED STOCKS

Among computer-oriented stocks there are real problems. Almost all of them doubled or trebled in the past year; and there is a broad belief that the computer-leasing companies may be substantially overpriced. We have screened four computer-oriented issues for possible doubling.

Barry Wright Corporation plateaued in 1967 with per share net of $1.01, same as 1966. In 1968-69 it should do better. It is actually an industrial company with strong computer overtones. It makes shock and vibration controls of rubber and steel; and components used extensively in metal-working industries, including the Vlier power-clamping system. These are rather traditional industrial lines. Glamour, however, is represented in (1) Wright Line, the largest manufacturer and distributor of accessories and supplies for computers, including Tape-Seal storage systems, and (2) Mathatronics, acquired in 1966, which makes and markets the original desktop computer, and offers several models with full-size computer features. New specialized models are going into production. Barry Wright common (797,670 shares outstanding December 1, 1967, traded on AMEX, may deserve the attention of gain-seeking speculators.

Computing & Software, Inc., is an energetic performer. Its common is listed on AMEX, with 1,182,599 shares outstanding at April 24, 1968. Of this, 47 percent is owned by Whittaker Corporation. The company's business is to provide governmental and commercial customers with computing service, information, programming and technical services. The government is the biggest customer, accounting for over 35 percent of 1967 sales. Net income is gaining rapidly and 1968 earnings should show a substantial gain over 1967. Computing & Software moved from OTC to AMEX in spring, 1968.

Graphic Sciences, Inc., has already been a dazzling performer. Its common stock was offered originally in 1967 at $10 a share, and under the April 18, 1968, prospectus $15 million of 6 percent debentures convertible into common at $43 were offered at par. Both issues were sensationally oversubscribed.

Graphic Sciences has two major fields of endeavor: the leasing of IBM computers, through its wholly owned subsidiary, GSI Computer Leasing Corporation (with arrangements to finance computer purchases quite largely on borrowed capital); and the assembling and marketing of the Graphic Transceiver. This machine, acquired from Arthur D. Little, Inc., will transmit and receive graphic communications via the conventional use of the ordinary telephone. Commercial uses may include transmission of advertising copy, proofs, layouts, photographs, and editorial copy in the printing and publishing industry;

transmission of weather-information maps and charts, drawings, business documents, billings, invoices, orders, identification; and in medicine, transmission of prescriptions, medical records, and hospital reports.

Because of its sophisticated equipment and the panorama of uses for the Transceiver, Graphic Sciences, Inc., has captured the imagination of computer-minded speculators. While Graphic Sciences common sells at a high price, there are many who believe it might go much higher. Capitalization is $19.4 million in long-term debt, followed by 942,380 shares of common, with three officers and directors owning, in total, over 50 percent. Graphic Sciences trades OTC.

Applied Dynamics, Inc. On December 27, 1967, 125,000 shares of this burgeoning company were offered publicly at $12. The stock was a sellout, and went promptly to $34, in the OTC market.

Applied Dynamics, Inc., is engaged in the development, production, and sale of computing equipment, for the solution of scientific problems. This equipment is in increasing demand in educational and government research and development laboratories.

The company produces general-purpose analog and analog-hybrid computer systems and components. Also, it frequently has responsibility for the sale and performance of hybrid systems composed of analog and digital computers interconnected.

The top quality and sophistication of Applied Dynamics are illustrated by (1) contracts received for computer assistance in the control of air pollution; (2) a new element, faster and more economical, enabling computers to do higher math; (3) a computer that simulates flying conditions in a supersonic air transport.

For the six months ended December 31, 1967, sales of Applied Dynamics were $2,555,905, creating net income of 13 cents a share versus 9 cents for the same period in 1968. We would expect a significant earnings gain in 1968, and believe the stock deserves a quality rating among early-phase computer-oriented equities.

ELECTRONIC-SCIENTIFIC COMPANIES

Some of the most dramatic market gains in the past two years have been recorded in the electronic-scientific category. Makers of electronic circuitry, communication systems, sophisticated instruments, medical devices, nuclear and oceanographic equipment will surely prosper in the coming year. Here are our candidates.

Sterling Electronics has been moving forward rapidly. Houston based, it started out and expanded as a distributor of electronic components and consumer electric products; in 1967, it had twenty-four stocking branches in fifteen cities. Growth has continued, and 1967 sales were $30 million, up $6 million over 1966. Net income in the same period was up almost 40 percent. Mergers are broadening the horizons of Sterling. Its Chemistron Corporation (Houston) produces printed circuits; Antenna Designs, Inc. (Burlington, Iowa), makes transformer coils; Henry Products Company (New York) manufactures sounding devices and electronic amplifiers; Hermetic Seal Corporation (61 percent owned) makes components and connectors. Other corporate units are Alma Radio, Index Geophysical Surveys Corporation, and a unit in computer services. Sterling is reported to be looking at a scientific company with unique skills in environmental chambers and specialized medical devices. At April 1, 1968, there were 833,373 shares listed on AMEX. Earnings appear to be in a rather pronounced upcurve. Sterling Electronics displays sturdy corporate momentum and has a sound management that has demonstrated vision.

United Nuclear Corporation is the only integrated fuel company whose business is exclusively nuclear. It provides everything "from ore to core," and ranks as the largest American miner and miller of uranium. It has, in total, about 590,000 acres of land in prolific Southwest uranium-prone terrain. As a fabricator, UNC produces nuclear fuel and complete reactor cores, supplying about 50 percent of the needs of the United States Navy's submarine fleet. Future earning power should be augmented by recent capital investments of $5.5 million in exploration, and $11.8 million in a new uranium-concentrating mill, to be ready in 1970. Viewing the rising global demand for uranium for military and civilian uses (electric-power reactors), and UNC's capability and resources in this field, we would look for a rising trend in its stock, which should earn $1.35 in fiscal 1969 (year ends March 31). United Nuclear is listed on the NYSE.

Damon Engineering, Inc., is only seven years old, and will cross $5 million in sales for the first time in fiscal 1968 (year ends August 31). Business is divided roughly into electronics, and educational and medical instrumentation. The electronics sector majors in quartz-crystal devices — filters, oscillators, and discriminators, and systems incorporating these — used in communications, missile control and tracking, sonar, and navigation. In education, Damon provides sophisticated equipment for new curriculum programs (principally science), distributed through the various publishers who turn out related textbooks. International Equipment Company, recently acquired, brings Damon into medical-laboratory equipment — centrifuges, cryostats, and cytoglomerators (for processing frozen blood). With IEC, Damon should gross $16 million in current fiscal year, and earn at least 80 cents on its 1,245,143 shares of common (OTC), against 39 cents last year. Management is young, talented, and profit minded.

Cavitron Corporation has displayed volatility. It moved from OTC to AMEX in April, 1968, and, accordingly, more speculators have been following it. Its ultrasonic dental unit has apparently been something of a breakthrough; it also produces a line of hand instruments for dentists; examining lighting systems for medical doctors, dentists, oculists, and veterinarians; monitoring equipment for jet aircraft; plus ultrasonic equipment for industrial use. The most recent feature is an instrument believed to be of benefit in the treatment of eye cataracts. Research may introduce, in due course, other advanced instruments. Small capitalization (635,791 shares), rising sales, and considerable glamour should continue to animate this one.

GCA Corporation, with 955,855 common shares, and listed on AMEX, is represented in research and/or production and systems for ballistic missiles, chemical and bacteriological warfare, undersea technology; vacuum technology in the treatment of exotic metals; capacitors, scientific equipment, and laboratory instruments, including monitoring equipment for the petroleum industry; data-identification instruments, and, most recently, by acquisition of Alpha Metals, Inc. This corporation is important in metal alloys and high-priority metals. Its earnings record is excellent. The company was sponsored originally by a group headed by Laurence Rockefeller. GCA has earned a profit in each year since incorporation.

Mark Systems, Inc., through continued research and development, has produced advanced techniques for recording information on film, and for retrieving that information. The company has achieved a total involvement in electric-photo optical technology, which equips it to meet the swiftly changing requirements generated by today's photo-optical revolution.

To reduce this scientific lingo to laymen's language, Mark Systems has perfected a processing that can take a succession of motion-picture shots, and produce a high-quality negative instantly. This processor uses Eastman Kodak Bimat transfer film. Mark Systems is also working with Stromberg-Carlson in connection with that company's micromation line of computer graphic read-out and retrieval.

The 1967 Annual Report revealed sales of $2,634,000, and net income of $226,000, or 36 cents per share. This is a good showing for a young company. For 1968, net should be 50 percent higher. About 977,000 shares are outstanding. This is an unusual speculation, wherein you rely on gifted management to create a significant company in a sophisticated scientific field. Stock trades OTC.

The romance in *Fifth Dimensions, Inc.,* is found in its Logcell, the registered trade name for a family of novel switching devices, based on a unique mercury film contact capsule. It is a basic component designed to fill the "gap" in switching elements between relays and semiconductor circuits. Its compact size, high speed, latching memory after power removal, and insensitivity to position shock and vibration are important attributes; and it has capacity to switch signals ranging from microvolts to several hundred volts, and currents from dry circuit to several amperes.

There are indications that Logcell may find broad applications in control instrumentation, computer networks, and communication circuits. If so, Fifth Dimensions, Inc., may reward those who speculate in the common stock. There are 578,280 shares outstanding, traded OTC.

Alloys Unlimited, Inc., began business in 1957 as a producer of high-purity, close-tolerance components for the semiconductor industry. Its growth and expansion have been on the spectacular side, with sales of $57.6 million for the fiscal year ended August 31, 1967. Eleven corporate subdivisions provide, variously, metal alloys, glass-to-metal seals, alumina ceramics for electronic miniaturization; electronic connectors; chemical milling; titanium products; coaxial connectors; shadow masks for color television tubes; and precision metal parts and assemblies. Over all, AU serves four markets: computer components, electronic appliances, micro-electronics, and aerospace. The company is constantly researching sophisticated new products and is an eager acquisitor. Management is technologically gifted, cost-conscious, and skilled in depth. The company's growth is outstanding — over 500 percent gain in earnings per share in four years. Current earnings are around $1.80 per share on 3.5 million common. A swinging stock, all AU has to do is maintain its historic market velocity in order to double again. It is listed on AMEX.

LIFE-INSURANCE SHARES

In the chapter on life insurance, we cited that industry for forward motion in 1968. The industry is growing at a rate of 7 percent a year; profits, assets, and earnings are at all-time highs. Life stocks, in the doldrums for four years, should advance in 1968-69. We like five companies.

Life Insurance Company of Kentucky would surely rate as one of the fastest-growing life companies in America — 27 percent compounded for the last five years. With only $74.3 million of insurance in force at the 1960 year end, LOK had ten times that at the end of 1967 — $752 million! In 1967 the company increased its assets 20.2 percent, its insurance in force 16.3 percent, and its total income 10.6 percent over 1966. Investment yield in 1967 was 4.91

percent, a rate that will surely increase in 1968 with available interest rates at historic highs.

Net profits of $547,333 for 1967 were $200,000 below the 1966 figure, due chiefly to non-recurring costs of about $300,000, as LOK prepared to market a combination of life insurance and mutual funds. This new sales package, coupled with LOK's low-cost computerized operation, traditionally aggressive salesmanship, and gifted management, should carry the company and the stock to new highs in the year to come. Only 1,567,720 shares are outstanding; it trades OTC.

National Liberty Corporation is an insurance holding company incorporated in 1967 to acquire all the capital stock of National Liberty Life Insurance Company, De Moss Associates, Inc., and Valley Forge Associates, Inc. According to a preliminary prospectus dated March 29, 1968, there were to be 3,801,000 shares of National Liberty Corporation outstanding after completion of the public offering of 400,000 shares (which took place July 2, 1968, at $15.00). The merging of these three corporations was designed to provide greater flexibility and to place the company in a position to consider or negotiate possible mergers in the future.

National Liberty Life Insurance Company had become a substantial company in the sale of individual accident, health, and life insurance. Its premium income in 1967 was $22 million, with 93 percent from accident and health insurance policies issued principally to persons who did not consume alcoholic beverages.

De Moss Associates, Inc., is a general insurance agency, engaged principally in soliciting business for National Liberty Life. Valley Forge Associates serves as advertising broker for both.

The stock of this quite new holding company may prove attractive to speculators partial to growing accident and health companies. Stock trades OTC.

United Benefit Life Insurance Company, with 500,000 shares outstanding, is a good doubling possibility. The stock earned $17.75 a share in 1967, without beefing up the figure by adding an amount for new life insurance written. Total assets are now $582 million, more than double the 1957 year-end figure. On a price/earnings ratio, United Benefit capital stock has to be rated as about the most attractive in the industry. Before a 5-for-1 split, this stock sold at $2,500 in 1964. At around $250, it appears a probable candidate for market ascension, another split, or a takeover. Mutual of Omaha already owns over two-thirds of this equity. It trades OTC.

Fidelity Union Life Insurance Company is one that should respond favorably to any upturn in the life-insurance market. Of companies with over $1 billion of life insurance in force, this one is the fastest growing. Its adjusted net per share has increased steadily from $3.13 in 1964 to $4.70 in 1967. At March 31, 1968, FULICO had $2 billion of life insurance in force. Its investment returns rank among the best, with 5.47 percent earned in 1967. Mortality experience has been favorable, averaging 36.6 percent since 1962. Over 84 percent of insurance is in whole life. The stock has just been split 2 for 1 and there are now 3 million shares outstanding. Here's a quality issue with far above average speculative potential. Mayflower Investment Company, a subsidiary, has substantial income-producing real property. With Mayflower included, 1968 net might be around $3 a share. It trades OTC.

Monarch Life Insurance Company is a rapidly growing company majoring in accident and health. This company is increasing its profits by about 9 percent annually and does a fine job of selling permanent life insurance with average premiums per $1,000 close to $20. Monarch, founded in 1901, should be a stellar performer in 1968-69. It trades OTC.

METAL SPECULATIONS

There are hundreds of gold mines in the United States and Canada, but a majority of them are shut down because the official price of gold ($35 an ounce) simply does not permit profitable production. Of $1.47 billion in gold produced in the Free World in 1967, the United States produced but $67 million. About 90 percent of all Canada's mines are subsidized by from $1 to $10 an ounce so that the gold-mining industry may stay alive.

If, however, the price of gold were advanced to $70 an ounce, which could happen in the next two years, gold stocks would soar. Accordingly, speculators should own some.

Dickenson Mines and *Camflo Mines* are two Canadian mines that we believe present the best values. Both are producing now, have good reserves, are well managed, and pay dividends. These are relatively low-priced shares traded actively on the Toronto Stock Exchange.

Kloof Mines, in South Africa (the world's largest gold producer), gets another of our votes. It's a young mine with large known reserves and might well become in a few years one of the world's great gold mines. Kloof common trades on the Stock Exchange in Johannesburg and OTC in the United States.

Charter Consolidated, Ltd., seems destined to become a widely popular speculation, and one of the great mineral companies of the world. There's plenty of stock available — 97.5 million shares traded in London, Paris, and Johannesburg on exchanges, and OTC in the United States, via American Depository Receipts.

Management is top flight: the company was put together in 1964 by the same people who run Anglo-American and De Beers Consolidated Mines, Ltd., and its chairman is the renowned Harry Oppenheimer.

Charter has a large-scale, global representation in major minerals and metals: gold, silver, platinum, copper, tungsten, zinc, nickel, and uranium. It is a big producer of gold and uranium in South Africa, of copper in Zambia, minerals and uranium in Canada, tin in Malàysia. It is astride the big nickel boom in Australia, and has substantial off-shore oil and gas holdings near England's south coast. Altogether, it owns thirty-one mining and/or banking houses, which have interests in portfolio investments worth (in today's market) over $600 million. In gold alone, Charter owns millions of shares in major South African producers, Western Deep Levels, and Western Holdings.

A company with such extensive holdings in natural resources, and enjoying one of the most sophisticated managements in the world, makes a logical appeal to those who seek rewarding hedges against inflation. Net profits of well above $30 million are possible in the year ending March 30, 1969.

Coeur d'Alene Mines appears to be a definitely favorable speculation in silver. Its properties are located in a region in Idaho that is rich in silver ores. The drilling and exploration is being shepherded and heavily financed by American Smelting and Refining, with profits, if any, to go 60 percent to ASARCO, and 40 percent to Coeur d'Alene. The company also owns 51.2 percent of Rainbow Mining and Milling, a substantial nearby silver property. If, as some have predicted, there is a rise in silver to $3 or $4 an ounce, Coeur d'Alene common is uniquely positioned to increase its earnings sensationally. It trades OTC.

THE CONGLOMERATES
Because conglomerates are in daily financial headlines, afford a wide diversity of investment within a single stock

certificate, and are so flexible in the securities they offer — bonds, preferred stocks, convertibles, and warrants — and have proved such rewarding speculations, we have selected three candidates.

National Industries, Inc., is a baby conglomerate that has displayed a lot of velocity. It has, in its corporate stable, La Salle Fire & Casualty; Southern Tank Lines, a Kentucky-based common carrier, operating in forty-five states, with a truck fleet of over 500 units for hauling dry and liquid cargoes; Kingswood Oil Co., an oil producer and liquid propane gas distributor; a large interest in Retail Centers of America, Inc., a mass-merchandising chain; a majority interest in Computer Research, Inc., operating data-processing centers; and 54 percent of Cott Corporation, which bottles soft drinks. Negotiations are reported with Crescent Corporation, and doubtless other projected acquisitions will be announced by the time this book is printed. If this snowballing conglomerate can shepherd all these units efficiently, then its stock may generate forward motion. There are 798,750 shares outstanding, closely held and traded on AMEX.

Automatic Sprinkler Corporation needs no introduction here. It was selected for doubling in 1967; and it did. As mentioned in the chapter on "The Corporate Hunter and His Quarry," Automatic Sprinkler is a hungry conglomerate with acquisitions on the fire on a year-round basis. The stock, after reaching 74 in January, 1968, fell as low as 27. In our view, it has the capacity to come back and possibly to star again in 1968-69. It trades on the NYSE.

Ebasco Industries, Inc., formerly Electric Bond and Share Company, was one of the dazzling utility holding companies of the 1929 era, and owned large blocks of Electric Power & Light Company, American Power & Light

Company, American Gas & Electric Company (now American Electric Power), and controlling stock in American & Foreign Power Company. Most of these holdings, except for American & Foreign Power, have since been sold.

The company has recently merged with American & Foreign Power, increasing its assets to about $440 million and will, in future, function not as an investment trust, but as a conglomerate holding company.

Its professional consultation services rank with the best, and at December 31, 1967, over 2,500 professionals —engineers, accountants, etc.—were at work on some 850 projects all over the world, with three service groups: Chemical Construction, Walter Kidde Constructors, and Ebasco Services, Inc. These top flight technical skills, plus some $60 million in marketable securities (not counting owned affiliates and majority stock ownerships in subsidiaries), place EBS in a position to make acquisitions, and to become perhaps a major conglomerate. Net assets of about $65 a share give EBS probably the highest ratio of book value to market price of any conglomerate holding company.

Speculators here can rely on management, renowned for three generations, a dividend of $2.00, and prospects for broad new corporate horizons and higher earnings, as the company is freed from the former restrictions of an investment trust. There are 6,798,987 shares listed NYSE. We expect them to perform well and possibly to double.

RANDOM SELECTIONS FROM
VARIOUS INDUSTRIAL GROUPS

Maine Sugar Industries, Inc., is a relatively new company endeavoring to build a new agricultural industry in Maine to supplement the concentration in the state on potatoes. From 3,300 acres planted in sugar beets in 1966, the acreage advanced to around 30,000 in 1967. Maine Sugar has a combination beet-cane sugar plant at Eastport, Maine. The company markets its sugar itself and also does some marketing through American Maize Products. By the end of 1968, the company hopes to sell 100 million pounds a year. In addition, Maine Sugar Industries leases farm equipment and machinery to farmers, and sells a special liquid fertilizer. The stock trades OTC with about 1.3 million shares outstanding. This is a special situation offering unique potentials for speculative gain.

Marion Laboratories is a successful ethical pharmaceutical company. Its drugs, including Pavabid for coronary and cardiac conditions, have gained wide acceptance. This year, Marion began marketing certain products developed by Syntex, including an interesting one for bronchial disorders. Two recent acquisitions, plus net profits rising probably over 50 percent in fiscal 1968, accompanied by expanding profit margins, give this stock luster, and genuine speculative attraction. About 2 million shares now trade OTC, but quite possibly the issue will be listed on the NYSE in 1969. Marion will have to work at it and split if it is to double, because it sells at so high a price. It has, however, the requisite dynamic qualities.

Goldfield Corporation is a mineral-oriented company that owns about 25 percent (over 400,000 shares) of General Host Corporation. General Host is a major American baker (Bond bread), producer and marketer of convenience and frozen foods and candy; owner of 41 percent of Uncle John's Restaurants and operates tourist attractions and facilities in Yellowstone and Everglades parks. Goldfield's Mining Division includes Getchell Mine, which was closed down in June, 1967, but may reopen if the gold price rises sufficiently. The company also has a

joint venture (in which it owns 60 percent) with Chem-
alloy Minerals, Ltd., and Tantalum Mining, Ltd., to develop tantalite deposits and production at Bernic Lake,
Manitoba. A 500-ton milling plant is now being built. Also
owned are a 50 percent interest in Canadian Potash Corporation, and 100 percent of Nucla-Power, Inc., a unit
for exploration of possible uranium deposits on over
500,000 acres in New Mexico. Copper claims are also
being explored in New Mexico. The major investment in
General Host, plus the romance and hopeful potentials
of all these mining projects, the aggressive management,
and the low market price, lend decided market attractiveness to Goldfield common. There are 7,844,000 shares
listed on AMEX. This stock has the price range, and the
diversity of profit sources, to make it a most popular
speculation.

Greater Washington Industrial Investments, Inc., is a
sort of conglomerate. It is a lively company, really a
closed-end investment company, organized in 1959 by an
energetic group of Washington, D.C., business and financial leaders to promote a source of venture capital for
scientific and industrial concerns.

Since formation, it has invested over $12 million in
forty-one scientific and industrial companies. GWII is
like an earlier stage of American Research and Development, which shepherded to public offering such companies as Ionics, Inc., Digital Equipment, Inc., and Applied Dynamics, Inc. GWII not only supplies needed capital, but makes available to satellite companies the technical and administrative experience and skills of its staff
and associates.

This company buys notes, debentures, or common
stock in young companies, receiving in most cases an 8
percent interest on indebtedness, and either a conversion

privilege for, or warrants to buy, common stock in the subject enterprise.

Portfolio investments as of December 31, 1967, totaled $4,982,980 in debt and equity securities at cost less reserves. Market value was over $17 million ($32.29 per share) with 31.9 percent in electronic communications, including radar, 28 percent in diversified technical companies, 17 percent in computer equipment (Data Products Corporation), and the balance spread over companies in electronic, instrument, drug, chemical, metal-working, software, optical, and technical-service companies. Its largest single investment ($4,586,625 at market value) was in 113,500 shares and $75,000 in 6 percent notes of Western Microwave Laboratories, Inc., of Santa Clara, California, maker of microwave devices and computer harnesses.

Under active guidance of Don A. Christensen, its president, GWII appears to be making impressive progress and building equity values for its 535,000 common shares. It is traded OTC.

Velcro Industries, Ltd., with plants in Manchester, New Hampshire, and Bramalea, Ontario, through wholly owned subsidiaries, makes Velcro fasteners under an exclusive license, covering nearly all the Free World, excluding Africa and Europe. This patented fastener is remarkable. It holds fabrics together by a pair of bands — one having hundreds of tiny hooks, and the other with an equal number of tiny loops. Just by pressing these bands together, a zipper-like solid fastening is achieved. The Velcro fastener has hundreds of uses in fabrics, medicine, furniture, automotives, carpentry, and decorating. Latest uses include paper dresses or surgical uniforms fastened by Velcro, all disposable. The future market for this unique product suggests that the company will continue to expand sales and profits at a rapid rate. A new plant, opened in 1967, notably expands production and increases efficiency. There are 3,216,000 shares trading OTC and quite closely held.

Medicenters of America common was publicly offered in 1966 at $10. The stock has since split 2 for 1 and was quoted around 40 OTC in May, 1968. This is a company formed to build and operate convalescent centers for in-patients and to license such institutions for others. Medicenters also has a construction affiliate for building centers for itself and licensees. The 270-bed Memphis Medicenter was opened last June; three others are being built. Six more wholly owned units are planned, and seven were licensed as of June 1, 1968. Expansion is the program of this company. The aim seems to be to generate rising income flow from owned units, and from fees, services, and profits from construction of units for licensees. Revenues of $2.7 million in 1968 are expected to expand in 1968-69, and to produce something more than the meager 2 cents a share reported at fiscal year end March 31, 1967. Outstanding are 1,261,000 common shares.

Medicenters is doing in the field of convalescent homes what Sheraton did in hotels, and Holiday Inns did in motels. It is building a chain of properties in several states, capable of earning above-average returns on capital by efficient, cost-controlled management, central buying, and standardized equipment and services.

Hexcel Corporation, serving the aircraft industry, is a leading specialist in honeycomb structures. Hexcel honeycombs have amazing strength-to-weight characteristics. They are made in cells (like a beehive) of aluminum, exotic metals, and even paper. All types of craft use this material — helicopters, rocket boosters, spacecraft, commercial and military aircraft; and each new model uses more than its predecessor. Hexcel should have 1968 sales of around $38 million, and per share net of close to $2, against $1.54 for 1967. About 1,040,000 shares are outstanding OTC. Acquisitions and new plants are widening future horizons. The boom in the manufacture of aircraft for the military, and the billions to be devoted to supersonic planes in the next five years, place Hexcel in the mainstream of a surging industrial market.

Mansfield Tire & Rubber is a major tire producer for the replacement market. It gave up a retail division of some 180 stores in 1965 and now concentrates on efficient tire and tube manufacture under its own brand names and under private trade names of such customers as oil companies, mail-order companies, and wholesalers. Its biggest contract is a ten-year-minimum one with Firestone, calling for the purchase of about 2.3 million tires in 1968, and a somewhat lower annual minimum in later years.

Mansfield's earnings for 1967 were a bit spotty, but in 1968 profit margins are improving, benefiting from an efficient new plant at Tupelo, Mississippi, with a capacity of 10,000 tires a day. With about 1.5 million of MSF common listed on AMEX, the issue does not have a large float. Earnings in 1968 may gain 40 percent or more over 1967. Also worth a look are the 5 percent subordinated debentures due in 1974, convertible into common at $22.24. The big propellant here is huge tire replacement demand created by the dynamic increase in the number of cars on the road each year.

Great Southwest Corporation has outstanding 1,133,132 shares of common preceded by $42.5 million in long-term debt, and 850,000 shares of $10 par preferred. The company is controlled by the Pennsylvania Company, an affiliate of the huge Penn Central railway system.

Great Southwest is a realty enterprise of stature and

promise. It owns, or has under lease, 6,600 acres of land making up the Great Southwest Industrial District between Dallas and Fort Worth, Texas. Here are already located over 225 companies in about 130 buildings. There is also an amusement park (Six Flags over Texas), a 308-room motel, a convention center, a golf course, and a beauty and health center. Additional land holdings include 70 acres in North Dallas, 3,000 acres in Atlanta, 1,000 acres in North Fort Worth, and eleven warehouses. As new companies move into these industrial acreages and build facilities, the earnings of Great Southwest should increase significantly. Furthermore, the land is so situated as to offer the probability of enhanced value over time. There is a relatively small floating supply of stock, traded OTC.

National Equipment Rental is one of the many leasing companies that have done well in the past two years. It is a lively company in this field, with a majority of its stock owned by American Export Industries. The company is engaged in leasing almost everything, including office equipment, data processing equipment, and airplanes. It is almost as eager for mergers as Litton.

The stock trades actively on AMEX. If you'd rather have a convertible than common stock, then consider National Equipment 5¼ percent debentures, convertible into common stock at $50. Both the bonds and the stock should be lively performers in the next twelve months.

KLM Royal Dutch Airlines is one of the great airlines of the world. A decline in earnings in 1967 dipped this aerial blue chip to the low 50's in early 1968. It would be our view that the decline in earnings here is past and that KLM common, listed on the NYSE, could well cross 100 this year and show net earnings of over $9 a share. This is essentially a rebound situation, and a rather conservative speculation on one of the best managed airlines, national or international.

Alpine Geophysical Associates is a scientific company with high competence in oceanography. Earnings from its technological fields have not, up to now, been dramatic, but it has enhanced considerably its total earning power by acquiring a fleet of tankers this year. This acquisition provides a large cash flow to Alpine and should exert a significant upward thrust to earnings. Alpine Geophysical, which trades OTC, appears an excellent candidate for higher market altitude.

Uris Buildings Corporation is one of the substantial and expanding equities in modern urban real estate. Its principal assets are ultramodern skyscrapers (some on leased and some on fee land) that are well located, splendidly tenanted, and virtually fully occupied. The skyscrapers are worth constantly more in terms of replacement value. New York holdings include 2 Broadway, 111 Wall Street, 320 Park Avenue, 850 Third Avenue, 1290 Sixth Avenue (jointly with Rockefeller Center), 245 Park Avenue, and 1301 Sixth Avenue. There's a joint venture interest in the New York Hilton and the Washington (D.C.) Hilton, as well as blueprinted projects in other areas. Uris both constructs and owns. Present properties total over 8.5 million square feet in rentable space. Their structures are designed to net the maximum profit per square foot, without too much regard for aesthetic values. The attributes of a valid inflation hedge make URB common attractive. There are 3,476,000 shares outstanding, listed on the NYSE, and some 800,000 warrants to buy 1.0609 shares of URB common for $12.50, good to 1975. The floating supply of common is small, as management owns over 65 percent. Earnings are rising, and cash flow via depreciation is impressive.

Norris Industries is a substantial company grossing around $250 million in 1968, whose common stock deserves a higher price/earnings multiple to reflect properly its growth and potentials. It started out as Norris Thermador, and changed its name in 1966. Through nine divisions and four wholly owned subsidiaries, Norris is engaged in the manufacture of a wide line of products for military, industrial, housing, and household markets. For the military, its Vernon Division makes bombs, projectiles, cartridge cases, and components for missiles and rockets. It supplies passenger-car wheels for the West Coast assembly plants of General Motors and Chrysler.

It is renowned for its consumer products, Thermador electric ranges, ovens, dishwashers, heaters, supplemented in 1967 by addition of the Waste King line, including ranges and garbage-disposal units.

Through diversification, military production is increasingly less important. Earnings are strong. We project per share net of about $2.30 on the 5.6 million common shares in 1968, and possible increase in dividend from present 80 cents. NRI common might sell much higher. It is listed on the NYSE.

There are four other speculative stocks, called to our attention just after this manuscript was completed, and too late for investigation on our part. We submit their names, without any documentation, leaving entirely to you the research as to their quality potentials, and their capacity to double, if any: *Asamera Oil Corporation*; *Metaframe Corporation*, the world's largest maker of aquariums; *Fuqua Industries*, a newer conglomerate; and *Jayark Corporation*, with a new portable projector.

45 NOMINATIONS FOR POSSIBLE DOUBLING
IN THE PERIOD FROM JUNE 1, 1968, THROUGH MAY 31, 1969

(Quotations Given as of May 31, 1968;
Either Last Sale or Closing Offering Prices)

STOCK	TRADED	PRICE
Alloys Unlimited	AMEX	43
Alpine Geophysical	OTC	38
Applied Dynamics	OTC	27 1/4
Automatic Sprinkler	NYSE	34
Barry Wright	AMEX	42 1/2
Canadian Homestead Oils	AMEX	5 7/16
Canadian Superior	AMEX	40 1/8
Camflo Mines	TORONTO	5.75
Cavitron	AMEX	47 1/8
Charter Consolidated	OTC	7 3/4
Clinton Oil	OTC	9 1/8
Coeur d'Alene	OTC	17 3/4
Computing & Software	AMEX	54 3/4
Consolidated Oil & Gas	AMEX	26
Damon Engineering	OTC	64 1/2
Dickenson Mines	TORONTO	4.80
Fidelity Union Life	OTC	47
Fifth Dimensions	OTC	12 1/2
GCA	AMEX	44 3/8
Goldfield	AMEX	10 7/8
Graphic Sciences	OTC	76
Great Southwest	OTC	92
Greater Washington Industrial	OTC	25 1/2
Hexcel Corporation	OTC	67
Hudson's Bay Oil & Gas	TORONTO	39
KLM Royal Dutch Airlines	NYSE	58 5/8
Kloof Mines	OTC	8 7/8
Life Insurance of Kentucky	OTC	20
Maine Sugar Industries	OTC	16 1/4
Mansfield Tire & Rubber	AMEX	24
Marion Laboratories	OTC	88
Mark Systems	OTC	50
Medicenters of America	OTC	49
Monarch Life	OTC	30 1/2
National Equipment Rental	AMEX	44 1/8

STOCK	TRADED	PRICE
National Industries	AMEX	25
National Liberty	OTC	15 1/2
Norris Industries	NYSE	32 3/4
Occidental Petroleum	NYSE	47 3/4
Sterling Electronics	AMEX	42 1/4
United Nuclear	NYSE	38 3/8
Uris Buildings	NYSE	38 3/4
United Benefit Life	OTC	251
Velcro Industries	OTC	64
White Shield	OTC	14

NOMINATIONS IN
CONVERTIBLES AND WARRANTS

We have not included, in our nominations for possible gains, specific issues of convertibles or warrants, for the reason that they are not stocks; and we set out specifically to describe in this book *stocks* that could double in a year. However, since we did have chapters on these hybrid speculations, we should not conclude without nominations in these categories. Accordingly, among converts, we suggest you investigate *Bohack 6's* convertible into common at $40; *National Equipment 5¼'s* convertible into common at $50; *Unexcelled 5¾'s* convertible at $38; *Loew's 5½'s* convertible at $90; *United Nuclear 5's* convertible at $40; *Mohawk Airlines 6's* convertible at $13; *Baxter Laboratories 4½'s* convertible at $42; *Automatic Sprinkler 4⅜'s* convertible at $60. These bonds, marginable at 50 percent, may generate worthwhile market gains in the coming twelve months. Check the current prices of each bond and stock after you read this. There are bound to be variations in market-price relationships by the time this book is in circulation.

Equally, there are some warrants that may produce

exciting results for you. Some with indicated promise are *Leasco* warrants to purchase common at $87; *Brun Sensor* warrants to buy common at $6; *Uris Buildings* at $12.38; *Ling-Temco* at $115; *Trans World Airlines* at $20; *Alleghany* at $3.75. Before making any commitment in warrants, check the relative prices of common and warrant, and take into consideration the expiration date of the warrant. If it has to gain 300 percent in price for you to break even in three years, you're probably paying too high a price for the warrant. Keep a lookout, too, for new warrants issued in acquisitions by lively companies. At the time this was written, *Fuqua Industries* was planning to issue warrants in part payment for a proposed acquisition. Check on these. In general, the best results are achieved by buying the warrant as soon as it is issued or becomes available in the trading market; and try to buy the warrant at ⅓ to ¼ (or less) of the market price of the subject stock. Buy warrants in rapidly growing, not static or fading, companies.

CONCLUDING OBSERVATIONS

Keep in mind that these stocks nominated for market action were chosen for special reasons. We hope, and rather expect, they will do well. Remember, however, that the information given about each is not comprehensive. Under no circumstances is it intended as the sole and final basis for making any market decision. Before even thinking about buying or selling these or any other stocks, you must get more complete and current information from a responsible source — brokerage house, investment counsel, investment service, or late prospectus or company report.

Nothing in this book is under any circumstance to be construed as a recommendation, endorsement, representation, or offer to buy and sell any security at any time.

All issues are mentioned as examples, for purposes of illustration, or as nominations in categories of securities with some possible expectation of price advance. We are solidly in favor of speculation but insist that you be an *informed* speculator — that you "investigate before you invest."

With this disclaimer, we are bold to say that speculation is great fun, is becoming intensely popular, and that trading in the stock market can add zest, adventure and an ever-changing panorama to your life — and perhaps make quite a bit of money for you.

However, remember that part of the trick in speculating successfully is knowing when to sell. Sell: (1) when your stocks reach a desired price objective; (2) when they fail to increase their earnings at expected rates; (3) using "Operation Baitback" — sell half when a stock has doubled and keep the other half free; (4) at the market, not at a specified price, which you may miss.

You may find that this book offers some guidelines to successful speculation. Its reading may inspire you to broaden your financial reading to include *The Commercial and Financial Chronicle, The Wall Street Journal, Forbes, Barron's,* the *Investment Dealers' Digest,* and the financial section of a metropolitan daily.

NEW HORIZONS

In addition to the 35,000 companies whose shares are traded or quoted with some frequency in the various marketplaces, the securities of new companies in new industries are constantly being offered. Obviously, none of these new offerings could be included in this book, since they are not yet in existence. It is important, however, that you keep on the lookout for new issues, as was suggested in the chapter on that subject, and more particularly, that you seek out in advance those rapidly growing and profitable industries from which new public offerings may emanate. These seem certain to include football clubs, mail-order schools, art galleries, employment and travel agencies, funeral parlors, candy-store chains, schools for elocution, memory, or investing. One of the most exciting industries to offer its shares publicly in the months ahead may be the brokerage industry itself. This is growing with amazing rapidity, and many exchange houses are increasing their business at the rate of 100 percent or more annually. The largest brokerage house, Merrill Lynch, Pierce, Fenner & Smith, Inc., added 203,000 new accounts in the first five months of 1968.

The market will continue to be, for the informed and the lucky, an exciting place for making money and adding excitement to life. Because of the millions of new stock buyers each year, and the quest for "performance" in mutual funds, stocks will turn over a lot faster, speculative swings will be wider and more frequent than ever before. Indeed, the climate for making and doubling money in stocks has seldom been more favorable. This book aims to make you better equipped to take advantage of these opportunities for stimulating trading gains.

In another decade, there will be 50 million stockholders, certificates will be done on computer cards, daily trading on the NYSE will average 30 million shares; and there will be $250 billion in mutual funds. Market operations will be almost completely computerized, to cope with the tremendous trading volume.

THE IMMEDIATE VIEW AHEAD

Decision to publish this updated book was made on the assumption that increases in federal taxes, rediscount rates, and margin requirements, occurring in the first half of 1968, would cause declining and possibly slow trading markets, lasting until autumn. A combination of three such regulatory actions in the past has always resulted in lower market prices for a few months thereafter. This year, market action has ignored these fiscal and monetary brakes. After the first quarter, stocks went into a strong upthrust, and trading volume on the exchange and over the counter has reached record volumes. At the manuscript deadline for this book, June 1, 1968, this market uptrend continues unabated.

Why is this bull market so unshakable? It must be because (1) so many people have so much surplus money to invest; (2) the hundreds of thousands of newcomers have watched others make money in the market, and are determined to do likewise; (3) stocks are scarce in relation to total demand; (4) the specter of inflation makes common stocks widely sought, as inflation hedges; and (5) corporate earnings are rising.

This roaring market shows no signs of slackening its pace. It might pause, or even decline moderately, should there be an end to the Vietnam war. This would create a temporary cutback of military production, and dislocations in readjusting our economy to increased civilian production. This period of changeover would not last long, however, and the full-scale devotion of our national material and human resources to building new homes, factories, roads, hospitals, urban rehabilitation, etc., would produce the most roaring economy we've ever seen. It could well carry our present bull market to 1,200 on the Dow-Jones Industrial Average.

In that event, the opportunities for market gain will be myriad, and many of the issues we have nominated may perform spectacularly. You will still need, however, five ingredients for your speculative success: money, information, judgment, courage, and patience. You'll also need a little luck. May 50 percent of your stocks double by June 1, 1969. In that event, *happiness* will indeed be *a stock that doubles in a year!*

index

index

ABOUT THE AUTHOR

IRA U. COBLEIGH is an economist who for the past eighteen years has been the feature and financial editor of *The Commercial and Financial Chronicle*. He is vice-president and economist of the DeWitt, Conklin Organization, Inc., a financial communications firm, and a director of five corporations. He is the author of a number of books that have sold, in total, over one million copies, including *Guide to Success in the Stock Market, How to Gain Security and Financial Independence, Expanding Your Income, Life Insurance for Financial Gains, and 100 Billion Dollars Can't Be Wrong*. A graduate of Columbia College, Mr. Cobleigh lives on Long Island with his wife, Dorothy. They have two sons and three grandchildren.